THE CATTLEMAN'S STEAK BOOK

THE
CATTLEMAN'S
STEAK BOOK

Best Beef Recipes by
CAROL TRUAX

Random Remarks and Rhymes by
S. OMAR BARKER

GROSSET & DUNLAP
A NATIONAL GENERAL COMPANY
Publishers · New York

A Castle Books, Inc. Edition
Distributed To The Trade
By Book Sales, Inc.

Published by
GROSSET & DUNLAP
Produced in Cooperation with
THE CATTLEMAN RESTAURANT
NEW YORK

The publisher wishes to thank the following for their permission to reprint the illustrations used in this book:

The Bettman Archive for pages 36 and 111;

Denver Public Library Western Collection for the endpapers;

Cooper Square Publishers, Inc., for page 9 (drawing by Joe De Yong) from *The Cowboy and his Interpreters* by Will James and others;

The Macmillan Co. for pages 1, 2, 5, 12, 34, 41 and 108 (drawings by Nick Eggenhofer) from *The Old Time Cowhand* by Ramon F. Adams, © 1961 Ramon F. Adams.

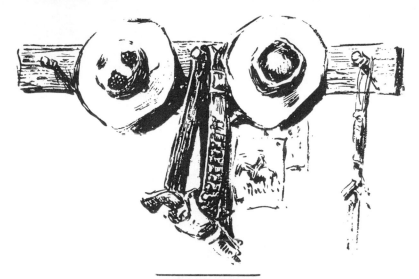

FOREWORD

It is significant to me that in our society of ever changing tastes, styles, and fads certain areas of life remain constant throughout the years. America's fondness for things Western is something that passes naturally from one generation to the next. Western music, literature, movies, fashions, and food never change yet they never seem to lose their broad appeal.

As proprietor of The Cattleman, a New York City restaurant with a Western motif, I am in a unique position to observe this phenomenon. The Cattleman, recapturing the charm and manly elegance of a plush San Francisco saloon or hotel at the turn of the century, has become one of the nation's most successful restaurants. Naturally, beef is its specialty, and it grills one thousand steaks a day, each prepared and served with a distinctive Western touch.

A beef dish can be as subtle or as simple as the palate demands. For this beef cookbook, The Cattleman and Carol Truax have collaborated on some of their choicest recipes. These recipes are shared with you in the hope that you will enjoy The Cattleman's brand of hearty, Western dining.

Larry Ellman
The Cattleman

Cattleman West
154 West 51st Street
New York, New York

5 East 45th Street
New York, New York

CONTENTS

THE
CATTLEMAN'S
STEAK BOOK

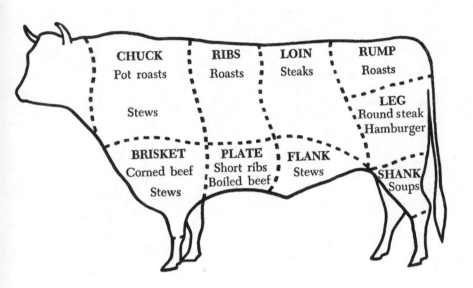

"Just think of all the money we'd make
If all our cattle would cut to steak!
We could well afford expensive feed
If we could raise an all-steak breed!"

Thus spoke a cowboy, young and bold,
And thus the Old Man got him told:

"Well, maybe the steak gets praised the most,
But the best brown gravy comes from roast;
And the kind of people are mighty few
Who don't enjoy a good beef stew.
Sure, *I* like steak, but I've also found
Good beef's still beef in meat loaf, ground.
The fact is, lad—and you won't deny it—
All cuts of beef are a he-man's diet.
And as for the women's appetite—
Beef suits them, too, when it's cooked just right.

"So never mind your all-steak breed!
Let's keep on a-raisin' what people need,
Here in this land where man's still free
To pick and choose his variety!
When it comes to cattle, let's just upgrade 'em,
Still in the pattern in which God made 'em!"

ADVICE TO BEEF-EATERS

First buy the beef.

The best way to buy beef is to talk it over with your butcher. Next to diamonds, a good butcher is a girl's best friend. Take your butcher's advice and your problems are solved.

But the old-time butcher's block is, alas, a vanishing piece of equipment. In supermarkets from Point Lobos to Penobscot, it has been replaced by a long refrigerator case full of cellophane packages. Today's beef buyers are on their own.

Good beef can still be recognized. It is richly marbled with white streaks where the fat that makes it tender shows. The color of the best-grown beef is a bright, clear crimson.

The best table beef is properly aged by hanging. Careful markets attend to this. It costs no more, and promotes customer satisfaction. The buyer will soon learn by experience whose beef is aged to the point of greatest succulence. She can see the marbled texture for herself through the clear cellophane.

All beef is government inspected, graded and labelled:

PRIME is the richest and most expensive. It is available in limited quantity.

CHOICE is the best buy for household use. It is of high quality.

GOOD is as nutritious as the better grades. It is less tender, and is of fair quality.

COMMERCIAL is tough, and needs to be treated with meat tenderizer. It is not recommended.

UTILITY is not suitable for household use.

CHOOSING A STEAK

Steak is the best food in the world. Everybody chooses steak. A good steak is the way to a man's heart. Overalls and white collars, chaps and gray flannel suits, they all choose steak. Steak stands for the good life in America.

Buying a steak by name is the neatest trick of the week. It depends on where you are.

London broil was never heard of in London. No one in New York knows what a New York Cut is. Ask an Iowan what a Top of Iowa steak is or try discussing a Kansas City steak with anyone from Kansas City. Every place has a different name for the same, or rather a similar, cut of beef. The actual butchering of cuts differs slightly from place to place. Retail beef cuts in different sections of the country vary somewhat, but the nomenclature varies a great deal.

Steaks go by the following names in the U.S.A.:

Porterhouse Steak	Boneless Sirloin Steak
T-Bone Steak	Strip Steak
Char Steak	Minute Steak
Rib Steak	Sirloin Strip Steak
King Steak	Delmonico Steak
Club Steak	Sirloin Steak
Shell Steak	Round Bone Sirloin
Hotel Steak	Pin Bone Sirloin
Top Loin Steak	Hip Bone Sirloin
Top Sirloin Steak	Top Loin Steak
New York Cut	Top of Iowa Steak
Spencer Steak	Family Steak
Kansas City Steak	Bottom Butt Steak

So you should have no trouble ordering a piece of loin steak if you: (a) know what you want, (b) know what it is called in your area, and (c) the butcher has any idea what you're talking about. It isn't only steaks that are planned to confuse you. What about a nice pot roast? Should you select:

Arm Roast	Skewer Roast
Shoulder Roast	Rolled Cross Rib Roast
Round Bone Roast	Round Muscle Roast
Flat Roast	Scotch Tender Roast
Chuck Roast	Round Roast
Blade Roast	Rolled Rump Roast
Seven Bone Roast	Triangle Rump Roast
Cross Rib Roast	Gooseneck Roast
Thick Rib Roast	Eye of Round Roast
English Roast	Sirloin Side Roast
Bottom Roast	Bottom Round Roast
Bread and Butter Roast	Face Rump
Neck Roast	Beef Shank
Shoulder Clod Roast	Boneless Brisket
Clod Roast	Bone-in Brisket

Are you sure you want a pot roast at all? In the "good old days" you just asked your butcher for a pot roast. It arrived, was cooked, eaten and subsequently paid for. Now, with a big case in a huge market filled with impersonal hunks of meat, it might be easier just to buy chicken. Honestly, we didn't make up these names. They were kindly supplied by the National Live Stock and Meat Board from Chicago.

All those names, however, were not supplied to confuse you, and they need not confuse you. That's where your butcher comes in. There is sure to be a good butcher somewhere behind the impersonal packages in the supermarket case. Ring the bell for him— not on a busy Saturday—and he will be glad to advise you. After a few such sessions, you will know what you want and how your butcher labels it.

Having chosen your cut, how many pounds shall you buy? For a rule of thumb, buy one-third to one-half pound of clear, bone-less beef per person. If you choose a steak with a minimum of bone, count on at least one-half pound each. If you are serving a roast like a prime rib with the delicious bones in, you will need almost a pound per person.

The best piece of steak is one and one-half to two inches thick. It is a mistake to sacrifice thickness to area.

It follows that two people cannot eat a sirloin steak, since a two-inch sirloin will weigh around five pounds. In buying steak for two or three, the best choice is strip, T-bone or filet. For four or five you might choose a thick porterhouse, and for a larger crowd, a big sirloin.

HOW TO COOK BEEF

No matter how perfect a piece of beef you choose, it can be spoiled in the cooking. Fortunately, the great American beefeater is becoming more sophisticated, more aware that a good steak or roast of beef is juicier, tastier and tenderer when it is not overcooked. People who used to demand beef well done now specify medium. The middle-of-the-roaders who liked medium now call for medium rare. Those who used to specify medium rare now come out for rare; and those who used to order rare now say, as the legend goes, "Drive it in and I'll bite it off!"

The safest way to decide if beef is cooked to the degree of doneness desired is to take its temperature. Put the meat thermometer into the center of the meat (not touching fat or bone). For rare it will read 130°, medium 140°, very well done 150°. You may test for doneness by making a tiny slit, near the bone, with the tip of a small sharp knife.

OUTDOOR COOKING

A man, by tradition, fancies himself a fire-maker and outdoor chef. To insure little or no trouble, you'd better lay the fire yourself and use briquets with some sure-fire spray or an electric lighter.

The fire should be started half an hour before cooking begins. When the coals are gray, shake off some of the ash and you're ready to go. If you have a persistent male cook, provide him with asbestos gloves and a pair of tongs, NO FORK, so the steak won't get holes punched in it to let the juices run out. Don't admit it, but a woman or a moderately bright child of either sex can cook the steak, provided you tell him or her the exact number of minutes to cook the steak. Don't, however, let several cooks go to work at once.

Hickory or other flavors can be obtained by adding a few dampened hickory chips to the charcoal fire, or by brushing the steak lightly with liquid smoke or sprinkling it with charcoal flavoring.

Of course you can also cook over a wood fire. Hickory, oak, maple and apple wood are all appropriate.

Other flavors can be imparted if you wish. Try adding a few bay leaves to the fire for the last five to ten minutes of cooking; or green fennel tops, dry fennel twigs, celery tops, parsley or herbs such as orégano or tarragon.

Don't make a huge fire, and don't let the fire get too high. If there are blue flames, probably caused by drippings, put them out by sprinkling with a little water from a bottle, a meat baster or a water pistol you have borrowed from your moderately bright child. Lacking a child, you can drop a small piece of ice out of your martini on the offending flame.

BARBECUING is usually done by smoke broiling over open heat. You must have a cover to smoke properly.

You can also barbecue in a covered pit, in a barrel cut in half and covered or in a smoke house.

However you do it, the barbecue is in the great American tradition, and fit for entertaining visiting royalty.

CARVING

When your beef is done, transfer it to a large, flat, warm platter. If you don't have a platter large enough to accommodate the whole roast or steak plus the slices you carve, provide a warmed plate to put the slices on.

Let a roast of beef stand, resting five to fifteen minutes before you carve it. A meat loaf should also rest a few minutes at room temperature before carving. Now pick up your sharp steel carving knife, and have at it.

Instructions are for right-handed carvers; if left-handed, reverse cutting left to right.

Standing Rib Roast: A two- or three-rib roast should be placed on its side on the platter with the bones to the left. Slice across the top of the roast from right to left. With the tip of the knife make a cut against the bones to release slices easily. If the roast is larger, it is preferable to stand it up on the bones and slice down from top to the bone. You will still need to use the tip of the knife between ribs and meat to release the slices easily.

Rolled Roasts: If small, the roast should be placed flat side down on the warmed platter and sliced across the top from right to left in pieces one-quarter to one-half inch thick. Lift each slice off before cutting another. Cut the string or cords as they get in the way. A larger rolled roast should be cut from top to bottom, the roast having been placed lengthwise on the platter. Start at the right end.

Roast Fillet is always placed on the platter the long way and cut in slices one-half to one inch thick.

Porterhouse Steak: Cut around all sides of the T-bone, loosen the meat from the bone and remove the bone. Then cut in slices diagonally across the whole steak. Don't throw the bone away; it's the tastiest piece!

Sirloin Steak: With the tip of a sharp knife, cut around the bones, freeing the meat. Cut across the whole steak in diagonal slices one-quarter to one-half inch thick.

Now enjoy your beef!

CAROL TRUAX

The color of a steer's hide don't matter,
Just so he's been well enough fed
For his fat to be white, his flesh just the right
Tender texture and healthily RED!

STEAK STEAK STEAK

Our cook was an ugly oldster
　By the name of Cranky Jake.
He done a heap of scoldin'
　But he savvied cookin' steak!
He made us cowhands step around,
　Mean as a rattlesnake.
He used a heap of cusswords
　But he sure savvied steak!
His pants was always saggy,
　His whiskers never neat,
But when it come to cookin' steak,
　He had the whole world beat!
His biscuits might be soggy,
　And he never fed us cake
But we et good at his wagon
　'Cause he savvied cookin' steak!

The man who savvies cooking steak broils it.

BROILING STEAK

Have the steak at room temperature for about an hour before cooking. Preheat the broiler; leave the door open while you broil to permit air circulation; if you close the door, you are baking rather than broiling. Broil a 1- to 1½-inch steak 3 inches from the heat, a 2- to 2½-inch steak 4 to 5 inches from the heat. For rare, broil 5 to 6 minutes on a side; for medium, 7 to 8 minutes; for well done (if you insist), 9 to 10 minutes.

To broil frozen steak, do not thaw but cook the steak 1 to 2 inches further away from the heat and cook about 2 minutes longer on each side. For a smoky flavor, brush with a little liquid smoke or sprinkle with charcoal flavoring before broiling. Do not prick the steak with a sharp fork; turn with tongs.

PAN-BROILING STEAK

Trim the excess fat from a sirloin, porterhouse or T-bone steak. If the steak is large, slit the edges of the fat. Heat a heavy skillet until sizzling hot and rub it lightly and quickly with a piece of steak fat stuck on a fork or sprinkle the bottom of the pan with a thin layer of salt. Put in the steak, sear for 2 minutes and turn to sear the other side. For a ½- to 1- inch steak, cook a total of 3 to 5 minutes on each side; a 1½-inch steak needs 8 minutes on one side, 6 on the other for rare. If the steak is thicker, reduce heat after the searing and cook about 10 minutes on a side. (A thin steak is better pan-broiled; a thicker one of 1½-inches or more is better broiled.) If using the salted pan, add freshly ground pepper and a little soft butter if you wish. If you don't use a salted pan, season with 1 teaspoon salt and ¼ teaspoon pepper after you cook the steak or salt each side as you turn the steak.

PAN-BROILED STEAK

6 individual steaks, ¾ to 1 inch thick (½ to ¾ pound each)
   club, Delmonico, shell or small T-bone; or 3 2-pound steaks
¼ cup butter   ¼ teaspoon pepper
1 teaspoon salt

Heat 2 tablespoons butter in a skillet. Sauté the steak 3 minutes, season with half the salt and pepper, then turn and season the other side. Cook 3 minutes on the second side. This should be rare. If you are not certain, do hesitate to cut a little slit near the bone with the tip of a sharp knife. Put the steak on a warmed platter or individual plates. Pour off excess fat. Scrape up all brown bits from the pan. Add remaining butter and pour over the steak, or serve in a warmed bowl or pitcher.   *Serves 6.*

OUTDOOR BROILING

Select a 2-inch steak. If you have a broiler with a hood and an adjustable grill, pile coals to one side, and sear steak for 2 minutes on each side, very close to the fire. Use a foil pan or make a foil trough to catch juices. Then raise the steak some inches above the heat, close hood and cook 10 minutes for rare, 12 to 15 for medium. If you don't have an adjustable grill, cook the steak several minutes less. Baste once or twice with juices from the steak and melted butter, mixed with a little wine or vermouth if you wish. Traditional barbecues have the sauce brushed on after the meat is done, or served on the side. You may brush with barbecue sauce while broiling if you wish. Season with salt and pepper after broiling.

Slim went to Kansas City with a freight train load of steers.
To such a rustic cowpoke with red and hairy ears,
The city seemed goshawful gay and sort of puzzling, too,
For the stockyards was the only place where he knew what to do.
Then a friendly cattle buyer sort of took ol' Slim in hand
And led him to a restaurant all flossied up so grand
That Slim's chin hit his brisket, and his eyes bugged out to see
The tables set with fufurraw and fancy fiddledee.
A waiter brought the menu, double-paged and two feet wide,
With a dozen fancy dinners on the printed list inside.
Slim read the list and pondered some, then kinder shook his head.
He grinned up at the waiter, and this is what he said:
"I've read your list of vittles and can say without a doubt,
I've never seen so much to eat that I can do without!
So tell the cook I'm sorry, but I reckon all I'll take
Is biscuits and some coffee and a slab of sirloin steak!"

BROILED SIRLOIN OR PORTERHOUSE STEAK

1 4- to 5-pound steak 1½ to 2 inches thick

1 teaspoon salt   ¼ teaspoon pepper
Soft butter (optional)

Slash the edges of the fat so the steak will stay flat while broiling. Preheat the broiler and broil about 3 inches from the heat until the top is well seared, about 5 minutes. Season with half the salt and pepper. Turn and cook on the other side for 4 to 5 minutes more for rare. You may wait to season until the steak is done. Smear with soft butter if you wish. If cooking over charcoal, be sure you have a good bed of coals showing a lot of white ash. Cook 3 minutes and turn to seal the juices in. Cook a total of about 6 minutes on a side for rare. The steak should be crisp outside and red or pink inside. Season. Add butter if you wish.   *Serves 6.*

CARPETBAG SIRLOIN STEAK

Sirloin 2½ inches thick (about 3 pounds boneless)

18 oysters   ¼ teaspoon pepper
1 teaspoon salt   2 tablespoons butter

Insert a sharp knife in the center of one side and make a cut to about 1 inch from the other side. Season the oysters with half the salt and pepper, put into the pocket, and sew up. Broil the steak for about 12 minutes on one side and 10 minutes on the other for rare. Season with remaining salt and pepper and brush with butter. For medium well done, cook 15 minutes on a side.   *Serves 6 to 8.*

CARPETBAG STEAK FILLETS

6 fillets about 2 inches thick

18 oysters   ½ teaspoon salt
¼ cup butter   ⅛ teaspoon pepper

Split each fillet, but do not cut all the way through. Make a pocket but keep the opening as small as you can. Warm the oysters in melted butter. Season with a little salt and pepper. Drain and put 3 in the pocket of each steak. Sew up the opening. Brush the steaks with the butter the oysters were warmed in and broil. Do not overcook—about 5 minutes on a side for medium rare.   *Serves 6.*

Much of the frontier West's indoor dining was done in hash-houses hastily set up in makeshift shacks, in wayside stagecoach stations, and in boardinghouse-style hotels, all without much swank or *beau monde* fixings.

El Dorado House in San Francisco was probably the first Western restaurant with prices high enough to be paid in gold. By contrast, for several years the Hotel de France, noted for filet mignon, served a five course dinner with a pint of wine, at a long family table, for fifteen cents. In the 1890's inflation pushed the tab up to twenty-five cents on week days, thirty-five on Sundays. There was no extra charge for making eyes at the barmaid.

TENDERLOIN OR FILLET OF BEEF

When cut one inch thick, this is a tournedos (served always in France); one-and-a-half inches thick, a filet mignon ('a "Frenched" filet mignon has a strip of bacon around the edge, fastened with skewer, toothpick or string); two-and-a-half inches thick, a Chateaubriand. Any larger piece is a beef tenderloin or whole fillet (filet).

FILETS MIGNONS

6 filets about 1 inch thick

1 teaspoon salt	6 slices bacon (optional)
¼ teaspoon pepper	Butter (optional)

Sprinkle filets with salt and pepper. If you wish to "French" them, put a piece of bacon around each and secure with a toothpick. Broil 3 inches from heat for about 3 minutes on each side for rare; 4 minutes for medium. Spread with a little soft butter if you wish.   *Serves 6.*

CHATEAUBRIAND (Broiled)

Piece of center-cut fillet (about 1½ pounds)

¾ teaspoon salt	4 tablespoons soft butter
¼ teaspoon pepper	

Sprinkle all sides of the beef with salt and pepper, and spread the top with 2 tablespoons soft butter. Broil for about 5 minutes on each side 3 inches from heat. Reduce heat, or put the steak in a 350° oven, and cook about 6 or 7 minutes longer. Spread with remaining butter and carve thin in diagonal slices.   *Serves 4.*

BEEF FILLETS IN BRANDY SAUCE

2 pounds beef tenderloin cut into 6 slices

¼ cup butter	1 teaspoon salt
1½ cups beef broth or	¼ teaspoon pepper
consommé	Sliced truffles (optional)
¾ cup brandy	

Sauté the beef in 2 tablespoons very hot butter for 2 to 3 minutes on each side. Put the meat on a hot platter and keep warm. Add broth, brandy, salt and pepper to the pan and boil to reduce it about half. Add truffles if you wish, cook a few minutes, remove and put with the beef. Add remaining butter, a little at a time, to the liquid and cook until blended. Pour over the meat.   *Serves 6.*

TOURNEDOS

12 1-inch thick slices from narrow end of tenderloin

3 tablespoons butter	¼ teaspoon pepper
1 teaspoons salt	Bearnaise Sauce° (optional)

Sauté the tournedos in hot butter for 4 minutes on each side for rare, 6 minutes for medium. Season with salt and pepper and serve on a heated platter. Serve 2 to each person.   *Serves 6.*

TOURNEDOS ROSSINI

Cook 12 tournedos as directed above. Place each on a round piece of bread, which has been sautéed in butter. Top with a slice of pâté de foie gras.   *Serves 6.*

"Man wants but little here below . . ."
For wives that's quite a break.
When feeling low, most any Joe
Will settle for a steak!

PEPPER STEAK

2½ pounds boneless sirloin steak 1 inch thick

2 tablespoons coarsely crushed peppercorns	2 tablespoons minced green onions
¼ cup butter	½ cup beef broth or consommé
1 tablespoon oil or rendered beef fat	⅓ cup cognac
1 teaspoon salt	

Rub the steak with pepper on both sides, pressing all of it into the meat. Let stand for an hour or two so the flavor will penetrate. Sauté the steak in 1 tablespoon each of hot butter and hot oil. Cook about 3 minutes on each side for rare, 4 minutes for medium. Season with salt. Remove steak to a hot platter. Add 1 tablespoon of butter to pan and sauté the onions for 2 minutes. Add the broth and boil to reduce. Add the cognac and let it boil down or, when it is hot, ignite. Remove from heat and add remaining butter a little at a time while stirring. Pour over the steak.   *Serves 6.*

PEPPER STEAK WITH WINE

2½ to 3 pounds boneless sirloin steak 1½ to 2 inches thick

2 tablespoons coarsely ground pepper	¼ cup olive oil
	2 tablespoons broth or water
1 teaspoon coarse salt	⅓ cup white wine
¼ cup butter	¼ cup brandy

Press the pepper into both sides of the steak; sprinkle with salt. Heat the butter and oil and sear the steak on both sides. Reduce heat and cook 5 minutes on each side. Put on a warm platter. Add broth and white wine to the pan juices. When hot, add the heated brandy and ignite. Pour over the steak.   *Serves 6.*

PEPPER STEAK WITH CREAM

2½ to 3 pounds lean fillet or top sirloin steak 1½ inches thick

2 teaspoons salt	¼ cup warm brandy
¼ cup peppercorns coarsely cracked	1 cup heavy cream
	Minced parsley
3 tablespoons oil	

Salt the steak, remove fat and bone and then press the pepper into the steak on both sides. Coat as heavily as possible. Brown in hot oil in a very hot pan for 2 to 3 minutes on each side. Remove steak and keep warm. Pour off some of the oil, leaving about 2 tablespoons of oil and drippings. Add brandy and ignite. Add cream and heat until thickened. Pour over the steak. Sprinkle with parsley.

Serves 6.

The porcupine, of solemn countenance,
Inhabits chiefly timbered mountenance
Where pine or spruce or fir tree bark is
The food that nourishes his carkis.

With quills his body is so prickly
That other beasts avoid him strickly.
Thus armed, the porky is defended
From tooth and claw, as God intended.

Though mayhap not the pork you pine for,
'Tis said that porky meat is fine for
You in case there comes occasion
When you are lost and face starvation.
Myself, for tasty porky roast,
I like this recipe the most:
First find your porcupine, then skin it.
Remove such innards as are in it.
Place on a smooth, selected plank,
Affix by lag screws, hip and flank.
Cook on a fire that you can trust
To ooze the juice and crisp the crust.
When done, remove and—hip and flank—
Throw meat away and eat the plank.
Thus porcupine, the beast incredible,
Is said by some to be quite edible.

PLANKED STEAK

1   2-inch T-bone, porterhouse, shell or club steak (about 4 pounds)
Garnishes

3-4 cups seasoned mashed
    potatoes
4-5 tomatoes, cut in half and
    seasoned with crumbs,
    salt and pepper, broiled
2 pounds peas or 2 boxes
    frozen peas, cooked
1 pound green beans or 2
    boxes frozen beans, cooked
3 cups slivered carrots, cooked

1 head cauliflower, broken
    into flowerettes, par-
    boiled
1 can tiny whole beets
1 can small whole onions
1 pound mushroom caps,
    sautéed 2 minutes in
    butter
½ cube butter
Juice of ½ lemon (optional)

Oil a plank of pine, oak or hickory about 10 inches by 15 inches by
1 inch (available in hardware stores). Heat the plank in a 400° oven
then place the steak in the center. Broil 4-5 minutes on each side. In
addition to the potatoes, choose from two to four of the vegetables.
Pre-cooked and seasoned, the vegetables should be arranged at-
tractively around the steak. The potatoes make a border around the

edge. Use a pastry tube with a large tip or spoon the potatoes close to the edge of the plank. Season steak with salt and pepper and spread with soft butter. Add lemon juice, if you wish. Place the plank under the broiler, not too close to the heat, and broil until potatoes are brown and steak and vegetables are hot. You may bake it in a 400° oven for 10 minutes, then broil close to the flame for 3-5 minutes.   *Serves 8.*

BEEF KEBABS

1½ pounds sirloin beef cut into 1-inch cubes

¾ cup soy sauce
½ teaspoon salt
¼ teaspoon pepper
¼ teaspoon garlic salt
12 small cooked whole onions
½ pound mushrooms

1 green pepper cut in 1-inch
   squares
2 not too ripe tomatoes cut
   in quarters or 8 to 12
   cherry tomatoes
¼ cup butter

Marinate the meat in soy sauce, salt, pepper and garlic salt for at least 2 hours, turning once or twice. Alternate on 4 skewers the meat, onions, mushrooms and green pepper. Put tomatoes on each end. Brush with melted butter. Broil 5 to 10 minutes on each side, depending on how you like your beef; brush several times with butter. Serve with rice or wheat pilaf.   *Serves 4.*

BAKED ROUND STEAK, ONIONS AND TOMATOES

2½ pounds round steak

1 teaspoon salt
¼ teaspoon pepper
¼ teaspoon garlic powder
3 tablespoons flour
2 tablespoons olive oil

2 cups thinly sliced onions
3 large tomatoes peeled and
   sliced
⅓ cup beef broth

Mix the salt, pepper and garlic powder with the flour and pound it into the steak on both sides—a heavy saucer is good for this. Brown the steak quickly on both sides in the hot oil. Put the steak in a casserole and brown the onions in the same skillet, adding a little more oil if needed. Spread the onions over the steak. Bake in a 350° oven for an hour. Add the tomatoes and broth and bake another 30 to 45 minutes until the meat is tender. Leave the cover off for the last 20 minutes of cooking. Adjust seasoning and thickness of gravy.   *Serves 6.*

GRILLED SALT-COATED STEAK

2½ to 3 pounds boneless sirloin steak 2 to 2½ inches thick
2 cloves garlic   Prepared mustard
Oil   Coarse salt

Crush the garlic and spread on steak. Brush with oil, spread with a thin layer of mustard and then cover both sides thoroughly with salt. Let stand for about one hour. Broil 3 inches from heat for 10 to 15 minutes on each side. Turn only once. To carve, cut the salt crust off and slice thin.   *Serves 6.*

BAKED STEAK

1   2-inch porterhouse steak
¼ cup olive oil   Paprika
¼ cup catchup   1 lemon sliced thin
2 tablespoons Worcestershire   ½ pound mushrooms sliced
     sauce   2 tablespoons butter

Mix the oil, catchup and Worcestershire sauce and pour over the steak. Let stand several hours, turning once or twice. Put into oven with the sauce and sprinkle with paprika. Add the lemon slices. Bake about 45 minutes. Just before serving, cover with the mushrooms, which have been sautéed in the butter.   *Serves 6.*

Those oldtime Western cowpokes
Missed a heap of stomach aches
By chompin' steak instead of guzzlin'
Fancy pies and cakes.
Of course they had their reasons,
And most of them admit it:
They rarely stuffed on cake and pie
Because they couldn't git it!

STEAK DIANE

1½-pound piece fillet or 2 pounds top sirloin
4 tablespoons butter   1 tablespoon chopped parsley
1 tablespoon chopped shallots   1 tablespoon Worcestershire
1 tablespoon chopped chives   sauce

Slice the steak thin (if using sirloin, trim off all the fat) and pound flat with a mallet. Heat 2 tablespoons butter and sauté the shallots until golden. Put in the steaks and cook quickly, a minute on each side. Add the chives, parsley, Worcestershire sauce and the remaining butter. Heat and serve.   *Serves 4.*

ESTERHAZY BEEF STEAK

2½ pounds boneless sirloin steak

¼ cup bacon fat and/or beef fat	1 teaspoon salt
2 onions coarsely chopped	¼ teaspoon pepper
2 stalks celery coarsely chopped	2 teaspoons paprika
1 small green pepper coarsely chopped	1 cup beef broth
1 tablespoon capers	2 tablespoons flour
	¼ cup sour cream
	2 to 3 tablespoons Madeira or sweet sherry

Have the steak cut into small neat pieces and flattened slightly. Heat half the fat and add the vegetables. Cook very slowly for 10 minutes. Add salt, pepper, and paprika and brown the vegetables. Add a few tablespoons of the broth mixed with the flour. Stir gently and add remaining broth. Meanwhile, sear the steak quickly in the remaining fat. Add steak to the vegetables and gravy. Stir in the sour cream and cook in a 350° oven for 20 to 30 minutes, depending upon the thickness of the steak.　　　　*Serves 6.*

SAUTEING STEAK

Steaks one-and-one-quarter inches thick or under are good cooked this way. Steaks one-half inch thick, often called minute steaks, are much better sautéed than broiled. Heat enough butter or olive oil, or a combination, to cover the bottom of a heavy skillet. Sauté over very high heat, turning once. A minute on a side is enough for a rare minute steak. If steak is one inch thick or a little more, reduce heat after searing on both sides and cook a total of three to five minutes on a side. If you wish to rinse out the pan with a few tablespoons of beef broth, water, red wine or cognac, do so and pour over the steak. Season with salt and pepper before or after sautéing.

To figure how hard the wind blows
　Out on the Texas Plains,
You hang a fresh-killed beef up
　With a pair of logging chains;
And if, on the morning after,
　You find your beef's been skinned,
And you have to ride to find the hide,
　There's been just a *little* wind!

GRILLED CHUCK STEAK

2 chuck steaks 1 to 1½ inches thick

1 onion minced
1 clove garlic crushed
¼ cup olive oil
2 tablespoons wine vinegar
¼ cup red wine

¼ cup catchup
½ teaspoon dry mustard
1 teaspoon salt
1 teaspoon meat tenderizer
⅛ teaspoon thyme

Mix the ingredients, except steak, buzz in a blender and pour over the steak. Marinate for 18 to 24 hours, turning the meat several times. Cook over charcoal or broil in the kitchen range for about 12 minutes if 1 inch thick; 15 to 18 minutes if 1½ inches. Baste with the sauce. Serve remaining sauce with meat.   *Serves 6.*

LONDON BROIL

1 large flank steak (about 3 pounds)

French dressing (optional)
1 teaspoon salt

¼ teaspoon pepper
¼ cup soft butter (optional)

Trim off fat and any tough membrane. You may marinate the beef in French dressing for 2 to 24 hours, turning it several times. Broil 3 inches from heat for 3 minutes on a side; this will be rare. London broil must be rare or it will be tough. Season with salt and pepper, and rub with the butter if you wish. Place on a warm platter or heated board and slice in thin slanting diagonal slices with a very sharp knife.   *Serves 6.*

FLANK STEAK STUFFED WITH MUSHROOMS AND CHEESE

1 flank steak (about 3 pounds)

½ pound mushrooms sliced
    or 2 (4 ounce) cans
2 tablespoons butter
2 tablespoons blue or Roquefort cheese

1 clove garlic crushed
1 teaspoon salt
¼ teaspoon pepper

Have the butcher make a pocket in the steak. If using fresh mushrooms, sauté for 2 minutes in 1 tablespoon butter; if canned, drain and sauté in the butter. Combine the mushrooms, crumbled cheese, remaining butter and garlic. Season with half the salt and pepper. Fill the pocket with this mixture and close with skewers. Sprinkle meat with remaining salt and pepper and broil 3 inches from heat for 3 to 4 minutes on each side. Place on a warmed platter and slice thin in diagonal slices against the grain.   *Serves 6.*

T-BONE STEAK

A T-bone steak, which is similar to a porterhouse but smaller, is excellent for individual servings or for two people. A two- to two-and-a-half inch steak, usually ample for two, may be broiled close to the heat for a total of twelve to fifteen minutes for rare to medium rare. Pan-broiling in a heavy, very hot, dry skillet is satisfactory. Turn the meat several times and pour off any fat that accumulates. This method takes a little less time than broiling. If cooking thin individual T-bone steaks, three-quarters to one-and-a-half inches thick, you may prefer to sauté them in a little butter or beef fat. Cook them over medium heat and watch them carefully, they don't take long.

MINUTE STEAK

4 steaks ¼ to ½ inch thick cut from sirloin (about 6 ounces each)
½ teaspoon salt ⅛ teaspoon pepper

Grease a hot skillet by rubbing it with a piece of fat from the steak. Cook over high heat 1 to 2 minutes on a side. Season with salt and pepper and serve at once. *Serves 4.*

MINUTE STEAK WITH SAUCE

6 cubed steaks or thin steaks cut from loin

3 tablespoons butter
2 tablespoons minced onion
1 teaspoon salt
¼ teaspoon freshly ground pepper

2 tablespoons minced parsley
1 to 2 tablespoons Worcester-shire sauce or A-1 sauce
¼ cup red wine

Sear the meat in very hot butter and remove to heated platter. Add all of the remaining ingredients except the wine and sauté over high heat for 2 to 3 minutes. Add wine, cover and turn down heat. When wine boils, pour the sauce over the steaks. *Serves 4 to 6.*

MINUTE OR CUBED STEAK VARIATIONS

Sprinkle the steaks with flour, brown well on both sides in butter or beef fat and add water to cover—about ½ cup. Cover and cook until fork tender.

Fry steaks quickly—1 minute on each side—in a dry hot skillet. Add ¼ cup butter and turn steaks to coat both sides. Remove to warmed platter, add a little salt and pepper to the butter, pour over steaks and sprinkle with chopped parsley.

CUBED STEAKS

4 large cubed steaks

Piece of beef fat   ⅛ teaspoon pepper
½ teaspoon salt

Heat a heavy skillet, rub it lightly with the fat, and sear the meat for a minute on each side. If you should happen to want it well done, cook another minute or two. Season with salt and pepper.   *Serves 4.*

SOUR MASH SKILLET STEAK

3 pounds top round sliced thin

1½ teaspoons salt
¼ teaspoon coarsely ground
    pepper
¼ pound butter
4 shallots minced
    Pinch dry mustard
1 teaspoon Worcestershire
    sauce

Dash Tabasco sauce
1 tablespoon brandy
1 tablespoon minced parsley
2 tablespoons brown gravy
    (commercial is satisfac-
    tory)

Cut the steak into about 18 pieces. Season with ½ teaspoon salt and pepper. Sauté for only a minute or two on each side in a very hot skillet just to brown the beef. Remove from pan and keep hot. Mix all the rest of the ingredients, except the gravy, into the butter. Put this mixture into the skillet and let melt. Add the gravy and heat. Pour over the steak pieces.   *Serves 6.*

Whenever Indians approached the trail boss of a northbound herd, and their leader held up one hand showing four fingers, and said "Wohaw!", the cowman knew exactly what he meant. He meant meat. It was a demand for four steers as the price for unmolested passage through or near Indian country. The demand might be for any number, or it might be pure bluff, but most trail bosses would strike the best bargain they could, pay the tribute and proceed with the herd unmolested.

A line in an old cowboy song has a cowboy singing to the cattle: "You'll be beef for Uncle Sam's Injuns." Once the plains tribes were located on reservations, Uncle Sam bought thousands of longhorns with which to feed them. In rationing out the beef, delivered on the hoof, the government agent would simply order a certain number of steers turned loose and let the Indians slaughter them on the run, as they had once slaughtered the buffalo. Maybe it was both cruel and unsanitary, but that was how the red man liked his wohaw —with plenty of wahoo!

SWISS STEAK

3 pound piece chuck or round steak about 1½ inches thick

1 clove garlic	½ cup diced carrot
1 teaspoon seasoned salt	1 teaspoon salt
¼ teaspoon pepper	½ teaspoon tarragon
½ cup flour	(optional)
3 onions sliced thin	½ teaspoon thyme
6 tablespoons shortening	(optional)
3½ cups consommé	½ teaspoon chives (optional)
½ cup diced celery	

Rub the steak with the garlic, seasoned salt and pepper. Sprinkle with the flour and pound in on both sides, using a blunt knife edge or the rim of a heavy plate. Try to pound in most of the flour. Brown the onions in the shortening in a heavy skillet and remove them to paper toweling. Add the meat and brown well on both sides. Return onions to skillet and add the consommé, celery and carrot. Season with the salt and herbs of your choice. Cover and simmer about 2½ hours until meat is fork-tender. Thicken the gravy with a little flour and water paste if you wish.   *Serves 6 to 8.*

STEER WITH BEER

2½ pounds round about ½ inch thick

½ cup flour	1 clove garlic (optional)
2 teaspoons salt	Parsley sprigs
¼ teaspoon pepper	⅛ teaspoon thyme
3 tablespoons shortening	1 bay leaf crushed
3 cups sliced onions	1 teaspoon sugar
1½ cups beer	2 tablespoons wine vinegar

Cut the meat into pieces about 3 inches square. Roll in flour which has been mixed with salt and pepper. Sauté in shortening until browned. Transfer meat to a casserole and fry the onions in the drippings. Add balance of seasoned flour and blend. Pour in the beer and bring to a boil. Pour this mixture over the meat. Add the parsley, thyme, bay leaf and sugar. Simmer until meat is tender, about an hour. Add the vinegar and cook another 15 minutes. Adjust seasoning to taste. If the liquid becomes too thick, add a little more beer or water.   *Serves 6.*

The "chaps" on a western ranch aren't the cowboys. They're those seatless leather pants the cowpokes wear to fend off the brush, to give their legs a better grip on saddle leather, to protect them from the weather, and to add cowboy style to their rigging. They also make a pretty good cow-driving noise when slapped with a rope.

You pronounce them "shaps," though gosh knows why, because the word comes from the Spanish *chaparreras,* meaning leather leggings, and pronounced *chah-pah-RRAY-rahs,* with plenty of *chuh* in the "*ch,*" and all the rolling of "*r's*" your tongue can wrangle. Some authorities claim the Spanish word is *chaparejos (chah-pah-RAY-hos),* and they may be equally right. Anyhow, it's hardly worth arguing over. As the cowboys say, "They ain't got no seat in 'em, either way!"

TENDERLOIN TIP CASSEROLE WITH MUSHROOMS

3 to 3½ pounds tenderloin tips cut into 1-inch cubes

Flour
2½ teaspoons salt
⅛ teaspoon pepper
2 tablespoons butter
1 cup chopped onions
2 cloves garlic crushed
1 pound mushrooms sliced

½ cup tomato purée
1 cup cream
¼ teaspoon Tabasco sauce
1 tablespoon Worcestershire sauce
1 cup sour cream

Dredge the meat lightly with flour, ½ teaspoon salt and the pepper. Brown quickly in the butter and transfer to a 3-quart casserole. Put in the onions and cook until tender. Then add the garlic, 1 teaspoon salt and the mushrooms. Cook 3 to 5 minutes, add the tomato purée, stir and pour over the meat. Bake, covered, in a 375° oven for half an hour. Heat the cream, Tabasco sauce, Worcestershire sauce and 1 teaspoon salt until simmering but not boiling. Fold in the sour cream and pour over the hot meat. Stir well and return casserole to oven for about 5 minutes until heated through. *Serves 6 to 8.*

OUTLAW SLICES OF STEAK

3 pounds beef flank or sirloin tip

¼ teaspoon garlic powder
1 teaspoon salt
½ teaspoon pepper

½ teaspoon paprika
½ teaspoon monosodium glutamate

Rub the meat thoroughly with a mixture of the seasonings. Broil about 10 minutes to degree of doneness desired. Slice diagonally. *Serves 6.*

STEAK IN WINE SAUCE

3 pounds round steak 1½ inches thick

2 tablespoons butter
3 onions chopped
2 tablespoons prepared mustard

½ teaspoon salt
¼ cup red wine
1 to 2 tablespoons flour

Brown the steak on both sides in butter. Add onions, mustard, salt, wine and ½ cup water. Simmer, covered tight for 2 hours. Add a little more water or a mixture of 1 part wine to 2 parts water if needed. Add flour to pan juices and simmer 3 minutes. Add a little more liquid if needed. *Serves 6.*

THE CHUCK WAGON

Most famous of all types of eating places in the Old West was a kitchen on wheels, its dining room as much of the adjacent outdoors as its patrons chose to occupy, seated crosslegged on the ground or squatting on their boot heels. Its patrons were cowhands, to whom it served three hearty meals a day as part payment for an honest day in the saddle working cattle, rarely less than twelve hours, often eighteen; for in those days cowboys rode "from mornin' can't-see to evenin' can't-see." This rambling range restaurant was, of course, the chuck wagon. Commonly just called "the wagon," it was of Texas origin but in general use for more than fifty years wherever Western cattle ranged.

On the earliest cow hunts in the longhorn country, each rider carried his own rations, usually cold biscuits, dry salt pork and sometimes jerky, in a sack tied on behind his saddle. On extended cattle gatherings a packed mule might serve as commissary, often with a Negro slave for cook. Either way, hot weather helped the salt pork get things pretty greasy; and to this day the term "greasy sack outfit" is sometimes applied to a ranch which packs chuck and camp gear on mules or horses into summer cattle ranges too rough for wagon, truck or jeep.

Successor to the greasy-sack commissary was a two-wheeled, ox-drawn, Mexican *carreta* used on roundups and the earliest trail drives from Texas to New Orleans. Even when four-wheeled, mule- or horse-drawn wagons came into use, the first ones were merely vehicles in which to haul camp gear and food supplies. There seems to be no record to tell us who first began stacking goods boxes in the tail end of the wagon for shelf room. But it does seem certain that a Panhandle-Plains pioneer cowman, Charles Goodnight, really invented the sure 'nough chuck wagon in the pattern that came to be pretty standard all over the cow country, all the way from Dilley, Texas to Dooley, Montana. The chuck box that Goodnight built in the tail end of the wagon bed was actually a cupboard about four feet high, with rows of drawers and shelves for cooking supplies and "eatin' tools." It had a slight forward slant, and its hinged lid was designed to drop down and serve as the cook's work table, which was further held level and steady by a scantling or pole brace from its underside to the ground.

A wide, deep shelf below the chuck box proper held Dutch ovens, skillets, kettles, coffee pot and other heavy cooking utensils. Usually a water keg rode on one side of the wagon box. On the other side was a long, deep box called "the hell box," which served to carry hobbles, pot hooks, sometimes branding irons, and all sorts of odds and ends of tools.

The wagon box itself held the main supplies of bacon or dry salt pork, flour, coffee, dried fruit, "lick" (syrup), and the sourdough keg. At times a quarter of beef might be added to this load, kept from spoiling for several days by wrapping in wet tarpaulin. In wet weather a wagonsheet drawn over wagonbows kept the chuckwagon's load dry. A dried cowhide, hammock-swung under the wagonbed was used to carry wood or cowchips so that the cook could always have at least some dry fuel for his cook-fire. This was "the cooney," from the Spanish *"cuna,"* meaning "cradle." It was also sometimes called the "possum belly" or the "skunk boat."

Whenever one wagon was not enough to haul all the bedrolls and supplies for a numerous roundup or trail crew, most outfits provided a second, lighter wagon called the "hoodlum wagon." In addition to his duties as *chef de cowcamp*, the cook drove the chuck wagon's four-horse or four-mule team—by no means a sissy assignment in a roadless country. The hoodlum wagon was driven by a helper called the roustabout or hoodlum, usually a teen-age kid a-hankering to be a cowboy.

Not only was "the wagon" the cowboy's boardinghouse, it was his home on the range—the only home he had during roundups and trail drives.

CARIBBEAN STEAK

3 pounds round steak 1½ inches thick

1 clove garlic minced or crushed
½ teaspoon thyme
½ teaspoon mace
½ teaspoon nutmeg
Few drops Angostura bitters

2 tablespoons minced parsley
2 onions sliced
1 teaspoon salt
¼ teaspoon pepper
¼ cup wine vinegar
2 tablespoons butter

Soak the steak in a marinade made of all of the ingredients except the butter. Turn steak once or twice and leave it for 2 to 4 hours. Pat dry and brown in butter. Add ½ cup water to the marinade and pour it over the steak. Cover and bake in a 350° oven for 2 to 3 hours until very tender. *Serves 6.*

Cowpunchers know the facts of life
As well as any man.
They know that beefsteak comes from cows,
And milk comes from a can.

BEEF STEAK AND KIDNEY PUDDING

2 pounds steak cut into 1-inch cubes

1 pound veal or beef kidneys
2 tablespoons flour

1 teaspoon salt
¼ teaspoon butter
Beef broth

Suet Crust

1 teaspoon baking soda
½ cup (scant) flour

⅛ teaspoon salt
¼ cup shredded beet suet

Remove the fat and membranes from the kidneys and cut them into about ½-inch pieces or slices. Roll the kidneys and beef in flour, which has been mixed with salt and pepper. Put into a deep baking dish with broth or water to cover. Leave at least ½ inch at top of dish. Taste for seasoning—it depends upon the broth. Make the crust by sifting soda with the flour and working in the suet. Add water a little at a time to make a soft dough—you'll use ½ to ¾ cup water. The dough should be springy to the touch, not too soft. Roll out and place on top, moisten edges and press on. Cover with waxed paper and then with a cloth; tie onto the top of the dish with string. Set the pudding in a kettle of hot water. The water should come ¾ up the outside of the dish. Cover and simmer for 3 hours. Remove cloth and paper before serving. Traditionally, a round of pastry at the top about 2 inches in diameter is cut out first and about a cup of boiling water added, for the sauce will be very thick. *Serves 6.*

STEAK AND KIDNEY PIE

2 pounds steak cut into 1-inch cubes

4 lamb kidneys
2 tablespoons flour
1 teaspoon salt
¼ teaspoon pepper

2 tablespoons butter or beef fat
1 onion chopped
1½ cups beef broth
½ cup red wine

Pastry

1 cup flour
¼ teaspoon salt

⅓ cup shortening
2 tablespoons ice water

Cut the kidneys into slices, removing fat and membranes. Roll beef in flour, mixed with salt and pepper. Brown in the butter or fat, add onion and brown 3 to 4 minutes. Pour into a casserole, add broth and half the wine and simmer covered for a half hour. Add remaining wine and the kidneys, which have been rolled in flour. For the pastry, have the ingredients very cold and handle as little as possible. Sift the flour with salt and cut in the shortening with a pastry blender or 2 knives until the pieces are a little larger than corn meal. Sprinkle on the water slowly, a tablespoon at a time, and toss with a fork until the dough will form a ball. Chill slightly. Then roll out on a lightly floured board to form a circle large enough to cover the casserole. Gash lightly to make steam vents and fit onto top of casserole. Cook in a 450° oven for 10 minutes, reduce to 350° and cook about an hour. *Serves 6.*

SIRLOIN STEAK AND KIDNEY PIE

2 pounds boneless sirloin cut into 1-inch pieces

¾ pound veal or lamb kidneys
2 tablespoons flour
1 teaspoon salt
¼ teaspoon pepper

2 tablespoons butter
Beef broth
Pastry (see recipe Steak and Kidney Pie)

Cut the kidneys into ½-inch pieces or slices, removing all fat and membranes. Roll the kidneys and beef in flour, which has been seasoned with salt and pepper. Brown in butter for a few minutes, add broth and simmer for 10 minutes. Cover with pie crust and bake in a 425° oven for about half an hour until crust is browned. *Serves 6.*

BEEF STEAK BISCUIT PIE

1½ pounds beef chuck cubed

Flour   1 medium onion sliced
¾ teaspoon salt   Dash monosodium
⅛ teaspoon pepper   glutamate
2 tablespoons shortening   ⅛ teaspoon nutmeg
¼ teaspoon basil   ⅛ teaspoon seasoned salt
½ teaspoon thyme   1 teaspoon Worcestershire
    sauce

Biscuit Dough

1 cup flour   2 tablespoons shortening
¼ teaspoon salt   6 tablespoons milk
1½ teaspoons baking powder

Roll the chuck in a small amount of flour seasoned with the salt and pepper. Sauté quickly in the shortening until golden brown on all sides. Add the basil, thyme, onion and 1 cup hot water. Simmer, covered, for a hour. Thicken with a paste made with 1 tablespoon flour and 3 tablespoons water. Season with monosodium glutamate, nutmeg, seasoned salt and Worcestershire sauce.

For the biscuits, sift the dry ingredients into a mixing bowl. Cut in the shortening until the mixture looks like corn meal. Add the milk all at once and stir together quickly until blended; the dough should be light and soft. Turn out on a lightly floured board, dip your hands in flour and knead the dough lightly and briefly—not more than half a minute. Pat or roll dough to ½-inch thickness and cut with a floured biscuit cutter.

Pour the meat mixture into a 1-quart casserole and place biscuits on top. Bake in a 400° oven for about 25 minutes until topping is browned.   *Serves 4.*

Some folks will eat just what they like—
A habit hard to break.
But cowboys like whatever they eat—
Just so it's steak!

THE GREAT AMERICAN HAMBURGER

Beef is beef and best is best,
And no other twain can top 'em.
That's how we like our steaks out West,
Whether you slice or chop 'em!

Ground beef is for everybody. Before you get your first tooth, and after you lose your last, tasty ground beef rolls richly in the mouth and goes easily down the gullet.

Ground beef is the most versatile of meats. From the homely meat loaf to the sophisticated steak tartare, it appeals to every palate. Hamburger is Europe's favorite American export. Good ground beef can be glamorized in a hundred ways.

Before it can be glamorized, it has to be good. Round steak, chuck, and flank are the best cuts for grinding. Buy it lean, and of a fresh, bright red color. Have it ground to order if possible, as it doesn't keep very well once it is chopped. It soon begins to get tired at the edges and lose its delicate flavor.

In preparing ground beef, keep it light and fluffy. Handle it as little as possible, and never pound it down or squash it flat in making patties.

HAMBURGERS

1½ to 2 pounds ground beef
1 teaspoon salt (scant)   Butter
¼ teaspoon pepper   4 hamburger rolls

Mix the meat with salt and pepper, tossing lightly. Form into 4 patties. Handle the beef as little as possible and make loose patties, not packed down. Sauté in 2 tablespoons very hot butter for about 2 minutes on a side for rare. Split the rolls and toast them. If you wish, butter them with remaining butter and put the meat on the rolls. You may serve catchup, mustard or relish on the side. The burgers may be broiled if you prefer; broil close to heat for 2 to 3 minutes on each side.   *Serves 4.*

HAMBURGER STEAK

Proceed as for Hamburgers° using 2 pounds of beef, but omit the rolls or buns. Serve on hot plates or a platter.

CHEESEBURGERS

1½ pounds ground beef
1 teaspoon salt   4 slices Cheddar cheese
¼ teaspoon pepper   4 hamburger rolls

Mix the beef with salt and pepper and make into 4 rather flat patties about the size of the cheese slices. Brown under broiler for 2 to 3 minutes, turn and brown the other side. Put slices of cheese on the patties and put under broiler until the cheese melts. Serve on plain or toasted hamburger buns.   *Serves 4.*

COWTOWN BURGERS

2½ pounds ground beef
1 teaspoon salt   12 slices toast
⅛ teaspoon pepper   12 thin slices Cheddar cheese
2 tablespoons butter or bacon   12 slices bacon cut in half
    drippings

Season the beef and form into 6 patties about 1½ inches thick. Brown on both sides in butter or bacon fat; leave very rare in the center. For each patty put 2 slices of toast on a baking sheet and cut the burgers in half; put a half on each slice of toast. Cover each with a slice of Cheddar and 2 half-slices of bacon. Bake in oven or broil until cheese melts and bacon is crisp.   *Serves 6.*

JESSE JAMES

The tale of Western outlaws would have to be the story of many different kinds of men, not all of it plumb gory. They had to eat . . . Most probably they figured beef was wholesome—at least there seems to be small doubt that, off and on, they stole some!

Of Jesse James so many claims to fame have been set down, that here we'll only mention one item of renown: whatever were his virtues, he robbed without remorse, and no other Western outlaw could excel him on a horse.

2 pounds ground beef

1 teaspoon salt	4 egg yolks
½ onion chopped	4 to 8 anchovies
¼ teaspoon pepper	

Season the beef with salt, pepper and onion. Make into 4 patties with an indentation in the center of each to hold the egg yolk. Broil or sauté to degree of doneness desired. Just before serving, place a yolk in the center of each. Served with half or whole anchovies over the yolk or with Anchovy Sauce*.   *Serves 4.*

BELLE STARR

Belle Starr was wife to Jimmy Reed, Cole Younger, and Sam Starr—a lurid lady outlaw whose fame has traveled far.

2 pounds ground beef

¾ teaspoon salt	4 slices Cheddar cheese
⅛ teaspoon pepper	4 slices tomato

Mix the meat with salt and pepper and form into 4 patties. If they are to be cooked quite rare, make them 1 inch thick. Sauté on one side for a very few minutes, turn over, place tomato on top and then the cheese. Either cook 3 minutes more and put under the broiler to melt the cheese or cover as soon as the cheese is put on and cook 4 minutes. If the burgers are to be well done or medium well, make the patties 1½ inches thick, split and put tomato and cheese between the split patties. Close up and sauté or broil.   *Serves 4.*

BILL DOOLIN

Bill Doolin, born in Arkansas, grew six feet two in height. He served in the Union Army, doing what he thought was right. Discharged at old Fort Stanton in the Lincoln county hills, he worked some as a cowpoke and traveled some for thrills. On a ranch in

Oklahoma, he was one of many hands laid off when landrush "Sooners" took over cattle lands. Without a job, he turned away from honesty and toil to organize an outlaw gang, and the pot began to boil. They robbed and stole until the law decided it must stop, and handsome big Bill Tilghman on Bill Doolin got the drop. The rest of Doolin's story is a sad one, so they say. They put him in the calaboose, from which he got away. Some say he died of illness, some say a shotgun blast was what turned Doolin's future into a buried past. Whichever way it happened, according to the song, Bill Doolin was a cowboy who happened to go wrong.

2 pounds ground beef

½ teaspoon salt	1 teaspoon thyme, basil or
¼ teaspoon pepper	oregano
1 tablespoon minced parsley	¼ cup tomato sauce
1 tablespoon minced chives, scallions or onion	

Mix the beef with the salt and pepper. Combine the remaining ingredients and fill 4 beef patties with ¼ of the mixture. Seal the slit through which the filling was pushed. Sauté or broil until cooked to the degree of doneness desired.   *Serves 4.*

BILLY THE KID

The fictional fame of Billy the Kid has spread both far and wide, but almost nothing that he did could be a cause for pride.

1½-2 pounds ground beef

½ teaspoon salt	4 slices Bermuda onion
¼ teaspoon pepper	4 slices Cheddar cheese
2 tablespoons butter	4 slices bacon cut in half

Season the beef with salt and pepper and form into 4 patties. Place in a skillet with the butter and brown for 2 to 3 minutes. Top each patty with a slice of onion and then a slice of cheese. Add 2 pieces of bacon, which have been sautéed for a minute or two. Put under broiler for a few minutes until the cheese melts.   *Serves 4.*

CLAY ALLISON

Clay Allison, when very young, was born in Tennessee. A soldier in the Civil War, he fought for General Lee. The Yankees took him prisoner, but he escaped one day, and headed west to Texas to earn a cowboy's pay. He helped to drive a longhorn herd out to New Mexico. 'Twas there he took up shootin', and his pistol wasn't slow. Oldtimers say he never stole but only loved to fight. He killed some men when he was wrong and some when he was right. He ranched awhile near Cimarron, a tall man, black of hair. They say he rarely killed a man whom most folks couldn't spare. The tooth a dentist pulled for him one time in Vegas town turned out to be the wrong one. Ol' Clay then got him down and yanked a half a dozen, and the way the story went, Clay never charged that dentist a single doggone cent! He lived somewhat by knife and gun, but died another way, when a wagon wheel ran over him and turned poor Clay to clay.

2 pounds ground beef

½ teaspoon salt	¼ pound Roquefort cheese
¼ teaspoon pepper	Cream (optional)

Season the beef with the salt and pepper. Smooth the cheese, adding a little cream if it is not soft. Make 4 patties of the beef and split each almost through. Stuff each with ¼ of the cheese and close the patties; seal edges with a little water or work with wet fingers. Broil or sauté to the degree of doneness desired.   *Serves 4.*

KID CURRY

Harve Logan, called "Kid Curry," was a bear for reading books; but he couldn't match the Sundance Kid for style and handsome looks.

2 pounds ground beef

1 onion minced	⅛ teaspoon pepper
1 to 2 teaspoons curry powder	Flaked coconut (optional)
½ teaspoon salt	Curry Sauce* (optional)

Mix the onion, curry powder, salt and pepper with the meat. Form into 4 patties about 1 inch thick. You may roll the patties in coconut or pat coconut on both sides. Sauté in a little butter or broil to degree of doneness desired. Serve with Curry Sauce if you wish.
    Serves 4.

BLACK BART

Black Bart, whose name was Charles E. Boles, was born in New York State. He served in the Union Army and came west rather late. About the '80's on the California coast, they voted Bart the outlaw that nobody liked the most. Blue eyes, gray hair, a big mustache, he didn't drink nor smoke, but every time he robbed a stage he'd have his little joke. One time when he had pulled a job, he left a little verse. It went like this (excuse me, folks, I only quote his curse): "I've labored long and hard for bread, for honor and for riches, but on my feet too long you've tred, you fine-haired sons-of-guns." They caught poor Bart and penned him up till 1888, and after they had turned him loose nobody knows his fate.

2 pounds ground beef

1 teaspoon salt	1 onion chopped
¼ teaspoon pepper	1 to 2 tablespoons butter
2 medium potatoes diced	

Season the beef with ½ teaspoon salt and the pepper. Brown the potatoes and onion in butter for 3 or 4 minutes and season with the remaining salt. Make 8 beef patties; place one-fourth of the potato mixture in the center of 4 patties. Cover with the other 4 patties and seal the edges. Sauté or broil to the degree of doneness desired

Serves 4.

SUNDANCE KID

2 pounds ground beef

1 teaspoon salt	½ cup chopped onion
¼ teaspoon pepper	1 tablespoon butter
½ cup diced green peppers	1 cup chili sauce

Mix half the salt and the pepper with the beef and form into 4 patties. Sauté the peppers and onion in the butter for 3 to 4 minutes, add the remaining salt and the chili sauce, and heat. Broil or sauté the beef to the degree of doneness desired and spoon the chili sauce mixture over the patties. *Serves 4.*

COLE YOUNGER

Cole Younger rode with Jesse James and Tulsa Jack with Doolin. Yep, those wild west lawless men were rawhide tough—no foolin'!

2 pounds ground beef

½ teaspoon salt	¼ pound Cheddar or Ameri-
⅛ teaspoon pepper	can cheese cut into bits
4 slices bacon	

Season the beef with salt and pepper. Make 4 patties and split each through. Fry the bacon and cut into bits. Drain off most of the bacon drippings and heat the cheese slightly in the same skillet. Mix cheese and bacon bits and put some in the center of each patty. Close up the patties; if you work with wet fingers, it's easier to seal the edges. Broil or sauté to degree of doneness desired. *Serves 4.*

JOHNNY RINGO

'Tis said of Johnny Ringo that he was educated—a sad-eyed man with auburn hair, in Arizona rated as one who'd fled from Texas with a price upon his head. On lonely ground, one day they found his bootless body dead.

2 pounds ground beef

1 teaspoon salt	1 cup canned or chopped
¼ teaspoon pepper	fresh tomatoes
1 onion minced	Pinch sugar
1 tablespoon butter	

Season the meat with ½ teaspoon salt and ⅛ teaspoon pepper. Sauté the onion in butter for 2 to 3 minutes. Add tomatoes, sugar and remaining salt and pepper. Simmer to reduce. Make 4 patties 1½ inches thick. Split the patties and put the tomato mixture between. Be sure to pinch the edges of the meat together so the sauce will stay inside. Broil or sauté in a little butter. *Serves 4.*

TULSA JACK BLAKE

A rawhide son was Tulsa Jack, whose maiden name was Blake. His lay-off from a cowboy job was more than he could take. He took out to the wild bunch, and he joined the Doolin Gang, as tough a bunch of outlaws as were ever meant to hang. But Tulsa Jack did not survive to stretch a sheriff's rope. He tried his best to do so, but the Fates decreed "no soap!" An Oklahoma train was robbed one night somewhere near Dover, and in a fight that followed, poor Tulsa's life was over. On May 5, 1895, the gun of Billy Banks wrote "period" to the story of poor Jack's lawless pranks.

2 pounds ground beef

½ teaspoon salt	1 large onion (preferably
¼ teaspoon pepper	Bermuda) sliced
2 tomatoes sliced	Mustard Sauce*

Season the beef with the salt and pepper. Make 4 patties and sauté or broil on both sides. Top with tomato, onion slices and Mustard Sauce. *Serves 4.*

WILD WEST

1½-2 pounds ground beef

1 teaspoon salt	2 tablespoons flour
¼ teaspoon pepper	¼ cup catchup
3 eggs slightly beaten	Hickory smoke (optional)

Mix all of the ingredients together. Add a few drops of liquid smoke or broil outdoors over hickory chips if you wish. Form into 4 patties 1 to 1½ inches thick. Broil for 2 to 4 minutes on each side.
Serves 4.

BARBECUED HAMBURGERS

2½ pounds ground beef

1 cup chopped onions	1 teaspoon salt
2 tablespoons chopped green pepper	¼ teaspoon pepper
2 tablespoons butter or fat	2 tablespoons sugar (optional)
½ cup catchup	1 tablespoon vinegar (optional)
2 tablespoons chili sauce	Toasted buns or toast
2 tablespoons prepared mustard	

Sauté the onions and green pepper in butter for several minutes. Add the beef and stir and cook until it browns slightly. Then add a mixture of the other ingredients and cook 2 to 3 minutes until thoroughly heated. Serve on toasted buns or toast. *Serves 6.*

On Western cow ranches where Papa the boss is,
He has his own choices of barbecue sauces.
He'll mix them himself so there's never a doubt
That plenty of *chile* has not been left out.

BARBECUED MEATBALLS

2½ pounds ground beef

1 teaspoon salt	1 teaspoon chili powder
¼ teaspoon pepper	2 tablespoons Worcestershire sauce
3 tablespoons butter or oil	
½ cup chili sauce	1 tablespoon prepared mustard
¼ cup wine vinegar	
2 tablespoons brown or white sugar	½ teaspoon liquid smoke (optional)

Mix the beef, salt and pepper and form into 1- to 1½-inch balls. Brown in butter or oil. Mix all of the rest of the ingredients, except the smoke, and bring to a boil. Brush the meatballs with smoke if you wish and add to the sauce. Cook for 10 minutes, stirring gently once or twice.   *Serves 6.*

ORIENTAL MEATBALLS

2 pounds ground beef

1 pound ground veal
2 teaspoons minced fresh ginger or ½ teaspoon powdered
1½ teaspoons salt
½ teaspoon pepper
1 onion minced

½ teaspoon agi no moto or monosodium glutamate
6 tablespoons soy sauce
¼ cup butter
3 tablespoons flour
1 cup beef broth
1 clove garlic crushed (optional)

Mix the beef, veal, half the ginger, the salt, pepper and onion. Add the agi no moto and 4 tablespoons soy sauce a little at a time, working them into the meat. Shape into balls the size of a walnut. Fry them, a few at a time, in 2 tablespoons butter, adding butter as needed. Transfer to a pan or casserole. Add flour to butter and drippings, brown slightly, add ½ cup water and the broth, remaining soy sauce, remaining ginger, and the garlic if you wish. When smooth and thick, pour over the meatballs. If using as canapés, make the meatballs smaller and serve the sauce on the side.

Serves 8 or makes 20 canapé servings.

SWEDISH MEATBALLS

2 to 2½ pounds ground beef

3 slices white bread
¾ cup water
1 onion minced
1 egg
1 teaspoon salt
½ teaspoon pepper

⅛ teaspoon nutmeg
½ cup flour
3 tablespoons butter
3 tablespoons broth, consommé or water

Break the bread into pieces and soak in the water. Add the onion, egg, salt, pepper, nutmeg and the meat. Blend thoroughly, using a fork to keep it light. Make into balls about 1 inch in diameter. Roll in flour and brown in butter, tossing the pan to keep the meatballs round. Brown a few at a time or use several pans. Put the meatballs together and add broth or water. Cover and cook very slowly for 20 minutes.   *Serves 6.*

SPICY MEATBALLS

2 pounds ground beef

2 cups soft bread cubes	1 teaspoon dry mustard
½ cup milk	3 eggs
1 onion chopped fine	1 clove garlic crushed
¼ cup butter	¼ cup flour
2 teaspoons salt	1 tablespoon tomato paste
¼ teaspoon pepper	1½ cups consommé
1 teaspoon nutmeg	1 cup sour cream
1 teaspoon paprika	

Soak the bread in water. Squeeze dry and add to the beef. Sauté the onion in 2 tablespoons butter and mix with salt, pepper, nutmeg, paprika, mustard and beaten eggs. Mix with meat and bread, toss with a fork and form into 36 to 48 balls. Brown in skillet, using remaining butter. Add garlic and use a little more butter if needed. Mix the flour with the tomato paste and consommé; add water to make 2 cups. Cook and stir until thickened, pour over meatballs and heat. Stir in the sour cream just before serving if you wish.

Serves 6.

So let's don't turn our noses up
At uncooked beef too hasty.
It's healthy chow, and anyhow,
Fixed right, it's mighty tasty!

SEASONED BEEF TARTARE WITH RAW EGGS

2½ pounds round, sirloin or rump steak (no fat) ground twice	
½ teaspoon salt	Dash Tabasco sauce
⅛ teaspoon pepper	6 eggs
1 tablespoon catchup	¼ cup finely chopped onion
1 teaspoon olive oil	2 tablespoons capers
½ teaspoon Worcestershire sauce	

Mix the freshly ground beef with salt, pepper, catchup, oil, Worcestershire sauce and Tabasco. Form into 6 flat round patties. Make a hollow in each large enough to hold a raw egg. Put the eggs in place and pile the onion and capers around the edge.   *Serves 6.*

BEEF TARTARE

2½ pounds ground sirloin or round steak
Garnishes

6 eggs or egg yolks	Minced parsley
½ cup minced onion	2 tablespoons caraway seed
¼ cup capers	Black caviar
¼ cup chopped dill pickle	Salt
6 anchovy fillets	Paprika
Minced chives	Pepper

Have the meat (no fat) double ground with fine blade. Use it as soon as you can after it has been ground. Handling as little as possible, gently make 6 round patties and with a wooden spoon make a depression in the center of each to hold the egg or yolk. Serve the egg yolk in its half shell or the whole egg in a small dish. Garnish the platter with a selection of the other ingredients in piles. Have salt and a pepper grinder available. Let each person mix his own tartare. He may omit the egg if he wishes and garnish to taste. Caviar is a lovely addition; you'll need at least ¼ pound. Omit anchovies and capers if using caviar. *Serves 6.*

MEAT LOAF

1½ pounds ground beef

1 onion chopped	½ teaspoon pepper
½ cup chopped celery	2 eggs
¼ cup butter	1 cup bread crumbs
1 small green pepper chopped	1 cup consommé
1 teaspoon salt	½ cup tomato juice

Brown the onion and celery in 2 tablespoons butter. Remove from heat and add the green pepper, salt, pepper, slightly beaten eggs and bread crumbs. Mix with half the consommé and add to the meat. Add balance of consommé and work it in until all is absorbed. Grease a loaf pan and fill pan with mixture. Bake in a 350° oven for half an hour. Mix the tomato juice with remaining butter, melted. Pour half of this over the meat, cook 15 minutes and then add the other half and cook 15 minutes more. Brown top under broiler if you wish. *Serves 4 to 6.*

Although plenty of pioneers of the Old West were "tough enough to chaw the hind leg off a kickin' longhorn steer," the fact is that mighty few of them habitually ate raw meat if they had any way to cook it. They had a good reason, not mere squeamishness. Even the best uncooked beef needs some "fixin's" to develop and bring out the innate flavor. And mighty few pioneers ever had the necessary condiments handy. Some of them might claim that they ate raw beef with the hair on when they had to or go hungry, but they also would admit that it "swallered better" if the hair was singed a little.

Indians, Mountain Men and buffalo hunters, however, were strong for fresh, raw buffalo liver, not only as a delicacy, but also as a health-food safeguard against scurvy, the coughin' collywobbles, the epizootic and various other similarly named ailments.

MEAT LOAF WITH HARD-COOKED EGGS

1½ pounds ground beef

½ pound ground pork
2 eggs
2 cups soft bread crumbs
2 tablespoons prepared horseradish
3 tablespoons catchup

1 tablespoon prepared mustard
¼ cup milk
1½ teaspoons salt
½ teaspoon pepper
2 hard-cooked eggs shelled

Mix the beef and pork with the slightly beaten eggs. Combine remaining ingredients (except hard-cooked eggs) and add to the meat mixture. Place half of this in a buttered loaf pan and make two depressions. Place an egg in each lengthwise and fill the pan with remaining meat. Bake in a 400° oven for an hour.   *Serves 6.*

RANGE LOAF

2 pounds ground beef

1 teaspoon salt
¼ teaspoon pepper
Pizza dough

1 (6 ounce) can tomato paste
½ teaspoon garlic salt
1 teaspoon dried orégano

Season the beef with salt, pepper, and garlic salt. You may make pizza dough from a hot-roll or bread mix if you wish. Roll it flat and cut into an oval or rectangle. Spread with tomato purée, sprinkle with orégano and place the beef in the center. Fold pizza around the meat, tucking in the edges. Bake in a 350° oven for about 40 minutes. You may make individual loaves by dividing the meat into 4 and placing on 4 pieces of pizza dough. Bake a few minutes less as the smaller portions of beef will cook faster. *Serves 4.*

MEAT LOAF WITH HAM

2 pounds ground beef

¾ pound ground flavorful ham	½ cup toasted bread crumbs
1 clove garlic crushed	2 eggs
1 teaspoon salt	½ cup consommé
½ teaspoon pepper	Bay leaves
1 onion minced	¼ pound bacon
½ teaspoon thyme	2 tablespoons melted butter

Mix all of the ingredients (except bay leaves, bacon and butter) very thoroughly. Keep mixing until liquid is absorbed. Line a loaf pan with six slices bacon and several bay leaves. Form the meat into a long loaf and put onto the bacon. Brush with melted butter and put 3 more slices of bacon over the top. Bake in a 350° oven for 1 to 1¼ hours. Baste with a little additional consommé if you wish.

Serves 6.

MEAT LOAF WITH CHEESE

2½ pounds ground beef

1 small can Virginia ham spread or ¼ pound prosciutto or Smithfield ham chopped	1 cup cracker crumbs
	1 egg
	¾ cup half-and-half cream
1 cup grated Parmesan cheese	1 teaspoon salt
	¼ teaspoon pepper
¼ cup chopped green pepper	1 small bay leaf crushed
½ cup chopped onion	½ teaspoon Tabasco sauce
¼ cup chopped parsley	¾ cup chili sauce

Mix all of the ingredients (except Tabasco and chili sauce). When thoroughly blended, put into a greased loaf pan and bake in a 350° oven for 45 minutes. Mix the Tabasco sauce with chili sauce and spread over the loaf. Bake 15 minutes more. *Serves 6 to 8.*

Absolute monarch of his chuckwagon domain and sometimes cranky, the cowcamp cook was no creative chef. When cowboys offered to buy Pothooks Perkins a cookbook, he squelched the idea right quick. "What the heck would I want with a cookbook?" he protested. "I already don't cook half as good as I know how!"

MEAT LOAF FOR TWO

¾ pound ground beef

1 onion minced	¼ teaspoon pepper
1 small green pepper chopped fine	1 teaspoon prepared mustard
2 tablespoons shortening, oil or bacon fat	1 teaspoon Worcestershire sauce
2 stalks celery chopped fine	¼ cup tomato juice
1 teaspoon salt	1 hard-cooked egg

Sauté the onion, green pepper and celery in shortening. When it starts to brown, add the salt, pepper, mustard, Worcestershire and tomato juice. Add the meat and mix thoroughly. Cool. Spread the mixture out and put the egg in the center. Roll up. Work with wet hands to insure enclosing the egg tight in the roll. Cover with a piece of oiled brown paper and bake for about 45 minutes in a 350° oven.

Serves 2.

CHILI MEAT LOAF

2 pounds ground beef

¼ cup minced green peppers	⅛ teaspoon ground chili pepper or cayenne
1 clove garlic crushed	
½ cup chopped onion	2 eggs
1 teaspoon salt	3 tablespoons broth
¼ teaspoon pepper	3 tablespoons bread crumbs
2 teaspoons chili powder	3 tablespoons butter

Mix the beef with green peppers, garlic and onion. Season with salt, pepper, chili powder and chili pepper. Beat the eggs lightly with the broth and work into the mixture. Form into a loaf and put into a baking dish. Sprinkle with buttered crumbs and dot with any remaining butter. Bake in a 350° oven for about an hour.   *Serves 6.*

BEEF AND NOODLES

2 pounds ground beef

1 cup chopped onion	½ teaspoon salt
2 tablespoons butter	¼ teaspoon pepper
3 cups wide noodles	1 tablespoon Worcestershire sauce
3 cups tomato juice	
1 teaspoon celery salt	2 cups sour cream

Cook the onion in butter until transparent. Add the beef and brown. Put raw noodles over the meat. Combine the rest of the ingredients (except sour cream) and pour over the beef and noodles. Bring to a boil, cover and simmer for half an hour. Stir in sour cream and heat but do not boil. *Serves 6.*

BEEF, RICE AND TOMATO CASSEROLE

2 to 2½ pounds ground beef

3 cups cooked rice	¼ pound mushrooms or 1
1 teaspoon salt	can (optional)
¼ teaspoon pepper	1 (10½ ounce) can mush-
1 onion minced	room soup
3 tablespoons butter	2 cups canned or stewed
1 clove garlic crushed	tomatoes

Put the rice in a casserole. Sauté the beef for 2 to 3 minutes with salt, pepper and onion in butter. Add this to the casserole with the garlic and mushrooms. Mix the mushroom soup with the tomatoes and pour over. Bake in a 350° oven for half an hour. *Serves 6.*

'Twas Christmas Eve out on the ranch, and all the winter crew
Was settin' 'round the bunkhouse fire with nothin' else to do
But let their fancies wander on the thoughts of Christmas chuck,
And what they'd like the best to eat, if they just had the luck
To set down to a table where the feast was laid so thick
That all they'd have to do was reach, to take their choice and pick.

Little Joe, the wrangler, claimed he'd love a stomach ache
From stuffin' steady half a day on choclit-frosted cake.
"A slab of turkey breast!" smacked Pete. "And good ol' punkin pie!"
"I'd reach for oyster dressin'!" Rusty Wilkins heaved a sigh.
"It ain't no Christmas feed for me," said little Jimmy Moss,
"Without brown turkey gravy and some red cranberry sauce!"
"Mince pie!" averred ol' Brazos Bill. "The kind my ma could make.
It beat your punkin forty ways, and also choclit cake!"

So each one named his fancy, till their chops begun to drip.
Then ol' Pop Slaughter give a snort and eased his crippled hip
By hitchin' to the window and a-sizin' up the night.
"Well, boys," he said, "it's Christmas Eve, and if I figger right,

That snow's too deep for travel, so before I hit the hay,
Upon the subject now in hand I'll kindly have my say:
It ain't what's in your stomack that's the most important part;
It's the feelin's in your gizzard, which is what some calls your heart.

"A-doin' others kindness is the road to Christmas cheer,
But that, of course, ain't possible, the way we're snowbound here.
It looks like all that we can do for our good Christmas deed
Is hustle all the livestock in and give 'em extry feed.
To hungry cows an extry fork of hay will seem as nice
As when a hungry cowpoke finds a raisin in his rice.
And as for fav'rite Christmas chuck, I'll name mine now, to wit:
It's beef and beans and biskits—*'cause I know that's what we'll git!*"

CHILI CON CARNE

1 to 1½ pounds ground beef

1 large onion sliced
3 tablespoons shortening or
    salad oil
1 green pepper chopped
1 (1 pound 13 ounce) can
    tomatoes
1½ teaspoons salt

3 cloves
1 bay leaf crushed
2 to 3 tablespoons chili
    powder
1 (1 pound 4 ounce) can red
    chili or kidney beans
½ cup red wine or water

Brown the onion in the shortening or oil. Add the beef and green
pepper. Brown, stiring as the meat cooks. Add the tomatoes, salt,
cloves, bay leaf and chili powder. Cover and cook about 2 hours.
Add the beans and wine or water. Simmer until heated through, about
5 minutes. *Serves 4.*

CHILI FAVORITE

1 pound ground beef

2 tablespoon bacon drip-
    pings
2 onions chopped
2 carrots grated
1 green pepper minced
2 (8 ounce) cans tomato
    sauce

1 teaspoon salt
¼ teaspoon pepper
½ teaspoon chili powder
1 teaspoon Worcestershire
    sauce
2 bouillon cubes
2 cups canned kidney beans

Brown the beef in the bacon drippings. Add vegetables, cook for
a few minutes and add the tomato sauce, salt, pepper, chili powder

and Worcestershire sauce. Dissolve the bouillon cubes in 1½ cups hot water and add to the beef mixture. Stir in the kidney beans and simmer for 20 minutes. Good served over rice.   *Serves 4.*

CHILI CASSEROLE

1 to 1½ pounds ground beef

4 slices bacon
1 cup thinly sliced onion
¼ cup chopped green
   pepper
2 (1 pound) cans kidney
   beans

1 cup canned tomatoes
   drained and chopped
2 tablespoons tomato paste
1½ teaspoons chili powder
½ teaspoon salt
¼ teaspoon cloves
1 clove garlic crushed

Cut the bacon slices into 4 to 6 pieces each and fry in a deep skillet. Add the onion and green pepper. Put in the ground beef, break it up with a fork and sauté until browned. Mix together the remaining ingredients. Combine with the meat mixture and mix well. Pour into a 2-quart casserole, cover and bake in a 300° oven for 1½ hours.   *Serves 6.*

QUICK CHILI CON CARNE

1 pound lean ground beef

1 large onion chopped
1 clove garlic crushed
1 green pepper shredded
   lengthwise
2 tablespoons bacon drip-
   pings or butter
1 (1 pound) can kidney
   beans drained

2½ tablespoons chili powder
1 cup canned tomatoes
   drained
1½ teaspoons salt
1 bay leaf crumbled
Dash cayenne pepper

Sauté the onion, garlic and green pepper gently for 10 minutes in the bacon drippings or butter in a Dutch oven, stirring occasionally. Add the meat and brown for 1 minute. Put in the kidney beans and lower the heat. In another pan mix together the chili powder and ¼ cup cold water and stir in the remaining ingredients. Bring to a boil and then pour this mixture over the meat and beans. Cover and simmer for half an hour.   *Serves 4.*

TAMALE PIE

¾ pound ground beef

1 cup corn meal	½ cup chopped pitted ripe
1½ teaspoons salt	olives
⅓ cup chopped green pepper	2 cups canned tomatoes
1 tablespoon shortening or	1 tablespoon chili powder
oil	½ teaspoon garlic salt
1 tablespoon flour	½ cup cubed sharp cheese

Bring 2 cups of water to a boil. Mix the corn meal with 1 cup cold water. Add 1 teaspoon salt and pour into the boiling water, stirring constantly. Cook until thickened, stirring frequently. Cover and continue cooking over low heat for 10 minutes. Cook the meat and green pepper in the shortening or oil in a skillet for 2 minutes until the meat is browned. Blend in the flour. Add the olives, tomatoes, chili powder, garlic salt and ½ teaspoon salt. Line the bottom and sides of a greased 6-cup casserole with the cooked corn meal. Fill with the meat mixture and sprinkle the top with the cheese. Bake in a 350° oven for half an hour. *Serves 4.*

TAMALE CASSEROLE

1 pound ground beef

1 (15½ ounce) can tamales	1 (6 ounce) can tomato paste
1 (12 ounce) can whole-kernel	1 teaspoon salt
corn or 1 package frozen	⅛ teaspoon pepper
2 small onions chopped	2 tablespoons grated Parmesan
2 tablespoons butter, shorten-	or Romano cheese
ing or bacon drippings	

Drain the tamales and save the liquid. Mash the tamales with a fork. If using frozen corn, cook and drain. Combine the tamales with the corn. Mix well. Break up the beef and brown in the butter in a hot skillet. Add the onions and cook a few minutes more, stirring frequently. Add the tomato paste and ⅔ cup of the liquid drained from the tamales. Season with salt and pepper. In a greased 2-quart casserole alternate layers of tamale-corn and hamburger-tomato mixtures. Sprinkle with cheese. Bake in a 350° oven for half an hour.
Serves 6.

The men who pioneered the West were eaters of meat—beef when they could get it, anything from "mule mutton" to mountain lion steak to baked beaver tail to peeled porcupine when they couldn't.

If there was a single vegetarian-on-purpose among those stalwart sons of adventure, his name and fame have long been forgotten. As one oldtimer remarked: "Ol' Nebuchadnezzar was the only man that ever et grass, and I've heard that he never did fatten very good on it." In fact, the Old West lived by the laconic saying: "Meat is Meat."

Still, if you stuff your meat into a sly vegetable now and then, the resulting dish does no harm, even if it doesn't "fatten very good" —which may even seem an advantage to some already stuffed beef-eaters.

STUFFED GREEN PEPPERS
1 pound ground beef

6 peppers	1 teaspoon salt
¼ cup butter	¼ teaspoon pepper
2 small onions chopped fine	¼ teaspoon cinnamon
½ cup rice	1 cup beef stock or con-
1 cup cooked or canned	sommé (optional)
tomatoes	

Cut tops from peppers and scoop out the seeds. Save the tops. Sauté the beef in 1 tablespoon butter for a couple of minutes; add remaining butter and the onions and sauté 5 minutes more. Add rice and sauté for 10 minutes while stirring. Add tomatoes, salt, pepper and cinnamon and cook for 3 or 4 minutes. Stuff the peppers with the mixture, put tops on to hold stuffing in and arrange in a baking dish. Add beef stock, consommé or 1 cup water and bake in a 350° oven for an hour.   *Serves 6.*

STUFFED PEPPERS WITH CORN
1 pound ground beef

6 large green peppers	2 eggs
½ cup chopped onion	1 cup whole kernel corn
2 tablespoons olive oil	1 (8 ounce) can tomato sauce
½ teaspoon salt	1 cup broth
¼ teaspoon pepper	

Cut the tops from the peppers and carefully scoop out the seeds. Sauté the onions in oil until transparent. Add the beef, salt and pepper and cook for 2 minutes only. Stir in the slightly beaten eggs and the corn. Stuff the peppers and put into a buttered or oiled baking dish. Mix the tomato sauce with the broth and pour over. Cover and bake in a 350° oven for about 45 minutes, uncover and cook half an hour longer.   *Serves 6.*

STUFFED GREEN PEPPERS WITH TOMATO SAUCE

1 pound ground beef

4 green peppers
1 teaspoon salt
¼ cup minced onion

¼ cup minced celery
1 egg
¼ cup cream

Sauce

2 cups canned tomatoes
¼ cup minced onion
½ teaspoon salt
2 teaspoons sugar

6 cloves
Pinch cinnamon
1 tablespoon flour

Cut a slice from the top of the peppers and remove seeds. Parboil the peppers for 4 to 5 minutes in salted water. Meanwhile, mix the beef, salt, onion and celery. Add the egg and cream. Toss all together and fill peppers with this mixture. Place in a baking dish. Make the sauce by heating the tomatoes, onion, salt, sugar, cloves and cinnamon together. Simmer 10 minutes. Strain. Reheat and thicken with flour mixed with about ¼ cup water. Cook until thickened. Pour over peppers. Bake in a 350° oven for about 45 minutes. *Serves 4.*

STUFFED CABBAGE

1 pound ground beef

1 large head cabbage
½ cup rice
1 onion minced
2 eggs
1½ teaspoons salt

¼ teaspoon pepper
1 (1 pound) can tomatoes
1 teaspoon lemon juice
2 tablespoons sugar

Pull off 12 large cabbage leaves and pour boiling water over them to make them easier to fold. Mix the rice, beef, onion, slightly beaten eggs, 1 teaspoon salt and the pepper. Put a mound (a twelfth) of the mixture on each leaf of cabbage. Roll, tucking in the edges, and fasten with a toothpick if you need to. Slice the remaining cabbage thin and put into a casserole. Put the cabbage rolls on top. Bring the tomatoes, lemon juice, sugar and remaining salt to a boil and pour over the cabbage. Cover and bake for an hour in a 350° oven. Uncover and cook another half hour. *Serves 6.*

MACARONI GOULASH

2 pounds ground beef

½ pound elbow macaroni
1 large onion chopped
2 tablespoons butter
1 teaspoon salt
¼ teaspoon pepper
2 cups canned tomatoes

1 (10¾ ounce) can consommé or beef broth
1 (10¾ ounce) can tomato soup
Buttered bread crumbs
¼ cup grated cheese

Cook the macaroni, wash with cold water and drain thoroughly. Sauté the beef and onion in the butter for about 3 minutes. Add the salt, pepper, tomatoes, consommé and tomato soup. Put the macaroni into a casserole and pour in the meat mixture. Bake in a 350° oven for half an hour. Top with crumbs mixed with cheese and put under broiler for a few minutes until browned.   *Serves 6.*

REDSKINS' BEEF STEW

2 pounds ground beef

2 tablespoons butter
1 medium onion chopped fine
1 green pepper chopped
3 tomatoes peeled and chopped
3 cups frozen corn or whole-kernel canned or fresh

1 tablespoon Worcestershire sauce
Dash Tabasco sauce
1 teaspoon sugar
2 teaspoons salt

Brown the beef in the butter. Add the onion and green pepper and cook 10 minutes. Add tomatoes, corn and seasoning. Cover and simmer 20 minutes.   *Serves 6.*

An Indian chief who likes lots of beef
 Remarked to his newly wed squaw:
"You want me to keepee same squaw in my teepee,
 You better cook plenty wohaw!"

CROQUETTES OF BEEF

1 pound ground beef

¾ cup cooked rice
2 large onions chopped
1 teaspoon salt

¼ teaspoon pepper
1 egg
½ cup oil

Mix the beef, rice and onions. Season with salt and pepper and stir in the beaten egg, which has been mixed with 3 to 4 tablespoons water. Form into 4 or 8 croquettes and fry in hot oil until browned.

Serves 4.

CHILI LONGHORNS

2 pounds ground beef

2 teaspoons chili powder
1 tablespoon minced green peppers
1 tablespoon minced red sweet pepper
1 tablespoon minced onion
1½ teaspoons salt

¼ teaspoon pepper
Cooked rice
1 (10¾ ounce) can beef gravy
1 (1 pound) can tomatoes
½ teaspoon garlic powder or instant minced garlic

Mix the beef with 1 teaspoon chili powder, the peppers, onion, 1 teaspoon salt and ⅛ teaspoon pepper. Shape into four cresents and broil to the degree of doneness desired. Serve on a bed of rice. Top with sauce made by simmering the beef gravy with tomatoes, garlic, 1 teaspoon chili powder, ½ teaspoon salt and ⅛ teaspoon pepper for about half an hour.

Serves 4.

ALAMO LOAF

2 pounds ground beef

1 green pepper diced
1 onion diced
1 pimiento diced
1 tablespoon minced parsley
2 tablespoons minced chives
¼ cup cooked rice
2 eggs
¼ cup catchup

1 clove garlic
⅛ teaspoon paprika
Pinch powdered saffron
⅛ teaspoon chili powder
1 tablespoon salt
¼ teaspoon pepper
Bread crumbs

Mix all the ingredients together and add only enough bread crumbs to absorb juices. Put into a greased loaf pan and bake in a 325° oven for 30 to 40 minutes. Serve with Hunter's Sauce*.

Serves 6.

THE CATTLEMAN'S
GOOD ROAST BEEF

The Spanish Captain General, Don Francisco Vásquez de Coronado, who came scouting the Southwest for the fabled Seven Golden Cities of Cíbola in 1540, seems to have realized that supermarkets with meat counters would be few and far between in *Nuevo Méjico*. To sustain the vim and vigor of his numerous entourage of *caballeros*, foot soldiers, and flunkies, not to mention his tame public relations man, Pedro de Castañeda de Nacera, he brought along rations-on-the-hoof: large herds of both cattle and sheep.

The Indians Coronado encountered were already familiar with the good red meat of buffalo, antelope, elk and deer, but this was their first look at domesticated cattle. However, they caught on quick. One of Coronado's many troubles on his long, hazardous and futile trip in search of non-existent Cíbola, was a natural tendency of the Indians to borrow a little tame meat-on-the-hoof whenever they got a chance.

Naturally the Spaniards also fudged a little on the Indians by killing some of their deer, antelope, and buffalo to supplement their dwindling supply of critters. Pedro de Castañeda failed to record whether or not they also cracked down on jackrabbits, but it seems doubtful that they would have bothered with bunnies as long as roast-size *carne* held out.

Coronado was not the first of the Spanish explorers. He only left more permanent tracks than Juan Ponce de León, who hit Florida in 1513 looking for the Fountain of Youth, and the ill fated expedition of Don Pánfilo de Narváez and Don Álvar Núñez Cabeza de Vaca in 1534. Meat-wise this latter expedition is notable for landing the first hogs in what is now the United States. You guessed it: the Indians found that they liked pork, too. It also happens that the second section of the name of one of these Spaniards, Cabeza de Vaca, means "Head of a Cow," not because he wore horns, but because one of his maternal ancestors was honored for guiding the army of Spain through a pass marked with the skull of a cow during the war with the Moors clear back in 1212 A.D. Shortened to C. de Vaca, more often C. de Baca, the name is still a frequent one in the Spanish-American Southwest.

This just goes to show how beef has always horned in on history, one way or another.

ROASTING BEEF

Do not wash the roast; it may be wiped with a damp cloth. It is roasted fat side up in a shallow open pan. Do not add water, do not cover. You may season with salt and pepper before roasting or after. Roast in a preheated 325° oven. A meat thermometer should register 130° for very rare, 135° rare, 140° medium, 150° medium well, and 160° for very well done. A four-pound roast takes from one-and-a-quarter to one-and-three-quarter hours; six-pound, two to two-and-a-half hours; eight-to ten-pound, two-and-one-half to three-and-one-half hours. Remove meat to a warm platter and let stand ten to fifteen minutes before carving.

A rolled roast is somewhat easier to carve, and more economical, but not as tasty and juicy as the king of all roasts, the prime rib.

Prime rib roasts are of the sets of seven or eight ribs. The first ribs are the choicer; the sixth, seventh and eighth are less tender, larger and have a little more waste. They should be (and usually are) less expensive than the choice first cuts.

The rump cut may be roasted by the foregoing method, or pot roasted. Other cuts suitable for pot roasting are chuck, round, shoulder or brisket.

If a drier cut like round is used for a roast, it should be larded and/or wrapped in suet by the butcher.

ROLLED RIB ROAST

5- to 6-pound rib roast boned and rolled
2 teaspoons salt   ¼ teaspoon pepper

Preheat the oven to 350°. Insert a meat thermometer in the center
of the roast. Season with salt and pepper and place in an open pan
with no water. Roast until the thermometer reaches 130° for rare,
140° for medium or 150° for well done. Remove from oven and let
the roast "rest" while you make gravy from the drippings. Skim off
excess fat. You may add a little flour and, if you wish, a little red
wine instead of water.

Another method is by low-temperature cooking in a very slow
oven (200°). The time will be approximately an hour a pound for
medium. Vary the time slightly up or down to reach the degree of
doneness desired. Test with the tip of a sharp knife or use a meat
thermometer.   *Serves 6.*

During a cattlemen's convention in Albuquerque, New Mexico, the
late Con W. Jackson, a leathery old cowman, found himself a guest
at a rather swank banquet. Noting that he seemed to be completely
ignoring his shrimp salad, the overly solicitous hostess expressed
concern about it.

"I'm so sorry, Mr. Jackson!" she chirruped. "I'm afraid you don't
like shrimps very well, do you?"

"Oh, I like the little boogers all right, ma'am," drawled the beef-
eating ranchman politely, "but just not quite well enough to eat 'em!
Not while there's roast beef around!"

ROAST FILLET OF BEEF

1 fillet of beef (3 to 3½ pounds)
Soft butter   Rosemary (optional)
1 teaspoon salt   ½ cup beef stock
¼ teaspoon pepper

Rub the fillet with butter, salt and pepper, and a little rosemary
if you wish. Roast in a 350° oven for about half an hour. Baste with
beef stock or broth and juices from the pan. (Cook a little longer
for medium well done.) Cut a tiny slit to check degree of doneness
if you wish. You may wait to season the beef until after it is cooked;
you may add butter at that time or omit it completely. Serve on a
warmed platter and carve ½- or 1-inch slices.   *Serves 8.*

ROAST LARDED FILLET

1 fillet of beef (3 to 3½ pounds)

| Salt pork or bacon | 1 teaspoon salt |
| Flour | ½ teaspoon pepper |

Lard the beef with salt pork or bacon, tie the thin end back and secure with string or skewers. Rub with flour. Bake in a 500° oven for 20 minutes. Baste often. Season with salt and pepper and let stand 5 minutes on a warmed platter before carving. You may roast it in a 300° oven for 30 to 40 minutes without basting. Carve in ½-inch slices. *Serves 8.*

FILLET OF BEEF BURGUNDY

1 fillet of beef (3 to 3½ pounds)

| Suet | 1 teaspoon salt |
| ½ cup burgundy | ¼ teaspoon pepper |

Have the butcher lard the fillet, or wrap with suet and tie with string. Broil for 15 minutes close to heat, turning once. If wrapped in suet, remove it. Next place the meat in a 250° oven for 20 minutes, basting with the burgundy. Just before serving, return meat to broiler for 5 to 10 minutes to brown. Pour the juices and wine over the meat. Season with salt and pepper. Carve in 1-inch slices. *Serves 8.*

BEEF WELLINGTON

(Filet de Boeuf en Croute)
3- to 3½-pound beef tenderloin

Flour	2 tablespoons cognac
1 teaspoon salt	2 tablespoons minced chives
¼ teaspoon freshly ground pepper	¼ cup paté de foie gras
1 tablespoon butter	½ pound puff dough (available at bakery)
1½ cups chopped mushrooms	2 egg yolks

Dust the beef with flour, seasoned with a little salt and pepper, and brown on all sides in butter. Remove the beef and keep in a warm place. Sauté the mushrooms for 2 minutes. Add cognac, chives and remaining salt and pepper. Remove from heat and mix with the foie gras. You may cover the fillet with the mixture or split the fillet lengthwise and spread the mushroom mixture in the center. Roll the pastry into a rectangle large enough to cover the beef. Put the beef in the center and wrap the pastry around it. Put the overlapping area on the underside. Fold the ends under, tucking them in tight.

Put onto a buttered baking sheet. Brush the pastry with beaten egg yolk. Bake for 20 to 30 minutes in a 350° oven. Let stand 10 minutes before moving very carefully to a warmed platter.   *Serves 8.*

Whether on roundup or trail drive, chuck wagon cookery was never elaborate. The cook was usually a former cowboy, either too old or too stove-up for cow work. Cooking over campfires in wind, rain or shine, the best he could do was to supply ten to thirty cowhands with plain food and plenty of it from a limited list of staples.

He fried bacon or dry salt pork (alias sow-belly or sow-bosom) and made gravy (alias cheap-and-easy or Texas butter). He boiled red or pinto beans (alias *frijoles* or Mexican strawberries) mellow enough not to rattle in the plate. He made pancakes (alias wheelers or splatter-dabs) to be eaten with syrup (alias lick or larrup). He stewed dried apples, prunes or apricots and sometimes bogged a few raisins in boiled rice and called it spotted pup (alias horse-thief special). He baked sourdough biscuits (alias doughgods or hot rocks) in a Dutch oven, and he kept a big pot steaming with coffee (alias Arbuckle's or brown gargle).

But the top item at the best wagons was BEEF (alias wohaw, or slow elk or big antelope if of questionable ownership). Sometimes stewed, more often roasted, most often fried, there was nothing like good beef to bolster a buckaroo's vim, vigor, and spizzerinktum, especially Dutch oven beef pot roast.

POT ROASTING BEEF

A pot roast is made from less tender pieces of beef such as rump, chuck, shoulder, round, sirloin tip or brisket. If using a lean cut (round or sirloin), have the butcher lard it with salt pork, bacon or suet. The piece of beef is browned in butter, oil or fat in a deep heavy pot, like a Dutch oven. Enough stock, water, wine or other liquid is added to make one-half to three-fourths inch in the bottom of the pot. It is then cooked slowly for several hours until tender. The liquid must be watched to maintain the one-half- to three-fourths-inch level. Gravy is made from the juices. You may dredge with flour before browning if you wish.

Another method is to dredge with flour and brown, add about three cups of liquid, cover and bake in a 300° oven, basting several times and turning the meat during the cooking period. This method will take a little longer than simmering over direct heat.

POT ROAST
4-pound piece rump, chuck, round or sirloin tip

1 clove garlic
1 teaspoon salt
¼ teaspoon pepper
Flour
½ teaspoon sugar
3 tablespoons fat, oil or
    butter

½ cup chopped onion
1 to 2 cups liquid: stock, red
    wine, or wine and water
1 bay leaf (optional)
1 teaspoon thyme (optional)

Have the roast trimmed and tied if necessary. Rub with garlic, salt and pepper. Roll in flour and, for easier browning, sprinkle with sugar. Brown thoroughly on all sides in a deep heavy pot. This should take about 15 minutes. Add the onion while browning. Pour 1 cup liquid over the meat. Add bay leaf, thyme or other herbs if you wish. Cover tight and simmer slowly 2 to 3 hours until tender. Keep the liquid about ½ inch deep in the pot, adding more as needed. If you wish to add vegetables, do so for the last half hour of cooking. Vegetables might include: carrots, turnips, small whole onions or larger ones quartered, diced celery or small potatoes.   *Serves* 8.

POT ROAST WESTERN STYLE
4-pound pot roast

2 teaspoons salt
¼ teaspoon pepper
3 tablespoons oil
2 cloves garlic minced or
    crushed

2 large onions chopped
2 cups dried prunes
1 cup pitted ripe olives
¼ to ½ pound mushrooms
    sliced or 1 (6 ounce) can

Rub the roast with salt and pepper. Brown in oil in a deep pot. Add garlic and onion and brown a few minutes more. Add 1 cup water, cover and simmer about 1 hour. Add prunes, which have been soaked in 2 cups water, with the prune water and olives. Cover and cook for about another hour until the meat is tender. Add mushrooms and cook 10 minutes longer. Remove meat to warmed platter and surround with the vegetables and fruit. Strain and thicken the gravy if you wish.   *Serves* 8.

Although flocks of sheep driven all the way from New Mexico constituted the first major meat supply for the thousands of miners of the California gold rush, it was not too long before the Forty-niners' demand for beef reached the ears of Texans in the longhorn country. The response was "beef, heap beef," as the old cowboy song puts it. There were fewer trail drives to the gold country than to Kansas, but it was to California that the largest trail herd in history was driven in 1869: 15,000 longhorns in four divisions, with a crew of 192 men, including cooks, and a *remuda* of 1200 horses. It is said that the mounted horns of some of those long-stepping critters may still be seen in an occasional tavern in the old gold country.

HERBED POT ROAST
4-pound pot roast

2 tablespoons fat or oil	1 teaspoon fines herbes
½ teaspoon powdered ginger or 2 teaspoons minced fresh	2 tablespoons minced parsley
	1 bay leaf
1 tablespoon sugar	1 teaspoon thyme
1 teaspoon salt	2 onions sliced
¼ teaspoon pepper	2 cups tomato juice or canned tomatoes

Brown the meat on all sides in fat in a Dutch oven or deep pot or casserole. Add all of the rest of the ingredients, cover tight and simmer for 2½ hours until tender. If the liquid gets too low, add a little water, broth or more tomato juice. There should never be less than ½ inch of liquid. If you wish, add some vegetables: a combination of small whole onions, small carrots or larger ones quartered, cut-up green peppers and/or celery, and potatoes; put these into the pot for the last half hour of cooking. Thicken gravy if you wish with a little flour and water paste.   *Serves 8.*

SPICY POT ROAST
3-pound pot roast

2 tablespoons oil or butter	2 cloves
½ cup minced onion	½ cup brown sugar
2 tablespoons mixed pickling spices	½ teaspoon cinnamon
2 teaspoons cardamon seed	1 cup vinegar
	2 cups stock

Brown the meat on all sides in oil or other shortening. Add onion and brown for a few minutes. Then add all of the ingredients, except the flour. Cover and simmer for 2 to 2½ hours until the meat is tender. Remove to a warmed platter. Strain juices if you wish. Add flour, mixed with a little water, and stir and cook until thick and smooth. Spoon a little sauce over the roast and serve the rest very hot in a saucebowl.   *Serves 6.*

SPANISH POT ROAST

3-pound piece of rump

1 teaspoon salt
¼ teaspoon pepper
Flour
2 tablespoons butter, oil or fat
1 (1 pound 4 ounce) can tomatoes or 5 fresh tomatoes peeled and chopped
1 cup beef broth or water and bouillon cube

2 tablespoons Worcestershire sauce
4 medium onions coarsely chopped
1 cup diced celery
¼ pound large mushrooms quartered
1 green pepper diced
3 carrots diced

Season the meat with salt and pepper and roll in flour. Brown on all sides in hot butter, oil or fat in a deep heavy pot or casserole. Add the tomatoes, the broth or water and bouillon cube and Worcestershire sauce. Cover and simmer for about 2 hours. Add the onions, celery, mushrooms, green pepper and carrots. Cover and cook another half hour until the meat is very tender. Thicken the gravy with a little flour if you wish.   *Serves 6.*

BOEUF A LA MODE

5-pound piece of beef (preferably rump)

2 teaspoons salt
½ teaspoon pepper
1 large onion sliced thin
1 stalk celery sliced thin
2 large carrots sliced thin
¼ cup chopped parsley
1 to 2 cloves garlic
1 bay leaf
½ teaspoon allspice
½ teaspoon thyme

2 cups wine
¼ cup olive oil
2 tablespoons beef fat, butter or oil
1 to 2 teaspoons sugar
2 cups beef broth
Cracked veal knuckle
Split calf's foot
Flour, cornstarch or arrowroot

Rub the meat with salt and pepper. Put about half of the vegetables and herbs in a deep bowl. Place meat on top of the vegetables and cover with remaining vegetables. Add the wine and oil. Marinate 24 hours, turning several times. Remove meat from marinade and pat dry. Brown it on all sides in hot beef fat, butter or oil. Sprinkle with a little sugar to assist in browning. Add the marinade and broth, the veal knuckle and split calf's foot. Cover tight and simmer in the oven or on top of the stove. Cook about 3 hours until tender, turning several times. If you want vegetables, add carrots and small onions for the last half hour of cooking; or cook separately, set aside and add for last 10 minutes of cooking. Put the roast on a warmed platter and surround with onions and carrots if you added them. Skim fat off the liquid and strain, pressing through a sieve. Thicken with a little flour, cornstarch or arrowroot mixed with a little red wine. Adjust seasoning to taste. Spoon a little sauce over the meat and serve the rest in a sauceboat. *Serves 10.*

BOEUF EN GELEE
(Made from Boeuf a la Mode)

This must be prepared some hours before serving, preferably a day ahead. Remove the beef from the pot after it is done and put it in a deep bowl with 1 cup of the broth to keep it moist. Strain and set aside the vegetables. Cool and skim off the fat from the remaining broth and chill in the refrigerator for several hours. Remove any remaining fat. If by any chance the broth has not jelled, add 2 teaspoons gelatin. Heat the jellied broth with the broth that was on the meat, strain through a cloth and let stand until syrupy. Cut the meat across —against the grain—in slices ¼ inch thick and place the pieces, overlapping, in a dish about 2 inches deep. Put the carrots and onions in the interstices. Slice or dice the meat from the calf's foot and sprinkle around the edges. Pour the syrupy broth over the whole. Return to refrigerator until the aspic is set; it should not be too stiff. *Serves 8.*

———————————

While meat rationing was in effect during World War II, a rancher was reported to the local Rationing Board for having several hundred pounds of fresh beef in his freezer. An official letter came soon thereafter, demanding to know what excuse the rancher could offer for having such a supply of beef on hand.

"Well, sir," the rancher wrote back, "I had to kill the whole steer at once or not at all."

The official involved was doubtless a first cousin of the Washington bureaucrat who took Laramie Luke severely to task for selling his entire herd of seventy-five steers.

"You must know, sir," the bureaucrat wrote sternly, "that it is the policy of this administration to provide for the future as well as the present. You should have retained at least twenty-five of your steers for breeding stock."

SAUERBRATEN

4- to 5-pound piece top round or sirloin

1 large onion minced and	12 peppercorns
3 onions sliced	6 cloves
1 tablespoon salt	2 bay leaves
1 teaspoon pepper	2 cups vinegar
Grated rind and juice of	1 to 2 tablespoons sugar
1 lemon	2 tablespoons flour

Mix the minced onion with salt, pepper and lemon rind and rub it into the meat. Tie the meat into a roll. Bring to a boil 2 cups water, the peppercorns, cloves, bay leaves, vinegar, sugar and lemon juice. Pour this hot over the meat and marinate in refrigerator for 1 to 3 days. Turn the meat twice a day. When ready to cook, place the meat in a deep casserole or roasting pan and pour the marinade over it. Add the sliced onions and cook in a 350° oven about 2 hours until the meat is tender. Place the beef on a hot platter and keep warm. Strain the liquid, skim off the fat and add the flour, made into a paste with a little water. Boil and stir for several minutes; adjust seasoning to taste. Spoon a little gravy over the meat and serve the rest on the side. *Serves 8.*

SAUERBRATEN WITH GINGERSNAPS

3-pound piece top sirloin

1 tablespoon salt	Celery tops
¼ teaspoon pepper	1 large carrot sliced
1 clove garlic crushed	3 to 4 cloves
2 cups vinegar	Flour
2 onions sliced thin	1 to 2 teaspoons sugar
2 bay leaves	5 gingersnaps

Have the meat rolled and tied. Rub with salt, pepper and garlic and place in a bowl. Add vinegar, onions, bay leaves, celery tops, carrot, cloves and 2 cups water. Cover and refrigerate for 1 to 3 days, turning a few times. When ready to cook, pat the meat dry and dust with flour. Sprinkle with sugar and brown on all sides in hot beef fat in a deep casserole. Add the marinade with the vegetables. Cover and simmer until tender, about two hours. Add a little more water if needed. Put the meat on a hot platter and keep warm. Strain the liquid, add the crushed gingersnaps and cook, while stirring, until smooth and thick. Pour a few tablespoons of sauce over the meat and serve the rest on the side. *Serves 6.*

ECUADORIAN BAKED BEEF

2½ pounds round cut 1 to 1½ inches thick

2 teaspoons salt
2 large onions chopped
1 green pepper chopped
2 tablespoons butter
2 tomatoes peeled and
    chopped or 1 cup
    canned

1 tablespoon paprika
¼ teaspoon pepper
¼ cup peanut butter
3 cups milk
6 potatoes peeled and cut
    into ½-inch cubes

Put the meat in a roasting pan with 1 cup water and 1 teaspoon salt and bake, covered, about 2 hours until tender. Fry onions and green pepper in butter until onions are light brown. Add tomatoes, paprika, remaining salt, pepper and peanut butter. Add the milk slowly. Simmer very gently for 10 minutes. Boil the potatoes in salted water. Place meat on a platter, surround with potatoes and pour sauce over all. *Serves 6.*

NEW ENGLAND BOILED DINNER

4- to 5-pound brisket of beef

1 small onion
2 cloves
1 carrot sliced
1 bay leaf
½ teaspoon rosemary
1 clove garlic minced
1 stalk celery or celery tops

Few sprigs parsley
8 potatoes peeled
8 carrots cut in half
8 small turnips
2 heads cabbage quartered
Beets (optional)

Put the meat in a large pot. Add the onion studded with cloves, the sliced carrot, bay leaf, rosemary, garlic, celery, parsley and water to cover. Cover, bring to a boil, reduce heat and simmer until tender, about 3 hours. Prepare the vegetables and add the potatoes, carrots and turnips. Simmer 15 minutes and add the cabbage. Cook 15 minutes more until the cabbage is crisp-tender. Slice the meat on a warmed platter and surround with vegetables. Beets, cooked separately or pickled, are traditionally served with New England Boiled Dinner. *Serves 8.*

The cow is of the bovine breed.
She cannot write, she cannot read.
What makes her even seem still dumber—
She won't give milk—we take it frum her.

The bull, her virile counterpart,
Has three strikes on him from the start.
As beef, his flesh is highly prized—
After he's been steer-ilized.

BOILED BEEF WITH VEGETABLES

3- to 3½-pound piece beef brisket or
3- to 4-pound piece cross rib beef

1 large onion sliced
2 stalks celery cut into 3-
    inch pieces
1 bay leaf crumbled
2 tablespoons vinegar

2 teaspoons salt
12 medium potatoes
12 small onions
12 small carrots

Put the beef in a deep stewing kettle or Dutch oven. Cover with boiling water. Add the sliced onion, celery stalks with leaves, bay leaf, vinegar and salt. Simmer gently for about 2½ hours until meat is almost tender. Add the vegetables and simmer about another half hour until the vegetables and meat are tender. Serve on a platter with the vegetables. Good with a horseradish sauce.

Serves 6 to 8.

"Barbacoa," the *vaqueros* of the Mexican Border called it. So did the Spanish-American descendants of the *Conquistadores* in New Mexico and Arizona. We *gringos* (no offense intended) appropriated the word and, as usual, worked it over a little to better suit the lingual limitations of our tongues and ears, hence "barbecue."

We not only borrowed the name; we also enthusiastically adopted the custom of cooking meat, especially beef, in considerable quantity, over covered coals in a pit dug in the ground. Pit-cooking was the original *barbacoa* of the *Mejicanos*. Nowadays almost any meat slow-cooked outdoors and not in a utensil is called "barbecue."

As world champion language makers, we *gringos* have also widened the linguistic scope of the original word considerably. *"Barbacoa"* is a noun and only a noun; but we have made "barbecue" serve also as a verb ("to barbecue"), and in its past participle ("barbecued") as an adjective.

In Old West writings it was sometimes spelled "barbeque," and several ranches on different ranges have used Bar B Q as a cattle brand. I once heard an old cowman remark that "it don't matter a hoot how you spell it, just so it makes you hungry when you smell it." And, properly prepared, it always does!

BARBECUING ROASTS

Cooking roasts out of doors is a pleasure, especially if you have a rotisserie. Standing or rolled ribs or a whole fillet need no advance treatment. Put them on the spit, be sure they are well balanced, and secure them with the prongs. They must turn only with the rod. Rump, chuck, arm roasts, any less tender cuts, need the meat tenderizer treatment, or you may soak them in a marinade for an hour or more. For any roast, keep the coals toward the rear and make a trough of aluminum foil to catch the juices.

Roasts cook faster by this method than in the oven. A rib roast needs fifteen minutes to the pound, less for rare, twenty to twenty-five for medium, with the meat four to five inches from the heat. Rump or chuck roasts need much longer cooking. Unless you are an experienced hand at this, a meat thermometer is strongly recommended.

They asked me, "What's a barbecue?" . . . I told 'em it's a feast
That fits the Western rangeland like a clam-bake fits the East.
When ranchmen want to entertain, they don't dress up in tails.
They put a man to choppin' wood, and send out o'er the trails
The word they're goin' to cook some beef on such and such a day,
And hope that folks will join them in a rangeland holiday.
When good prime beef gets roasted in a pit dug in the earth,
It may be meant to celebrate a weddin' or a birth.
A new ranch house completed or a mortgage paid in full,
Or just the recent purchase of a purebred Hereford bull.
In fact an ol' ranch barbecue don't need no more excuse
That just some rancher's feelin' that he'd like to cut 'er loose
And let his friends and neighbors know he's got the beef
    and wood
To celebrate a little when the grass is lookin' good.

There ain't no class distinction at a Western barbecue:
Bank presidents and cowboys git the same *wohaw* to chew.

The coffee and the pickles, like the welcome and the shade,
Are just as free to millionaires as them that plies a trade.
There ain't no rules of etiquette on how to set or squat,
Except that at a barbecue all feuds must be forgot.
It's said that them ol' Texans, who are rawhide-jawed and tough,
Will barbecue most anything that stands still long enough!
But ranchmen down in Texas, same as elsewhere in the West,
They butcher out to barbecue their fattest and their best.
It's beef with all the fixin's, but no matter what their name,
Nobody at a barbecue is sorry that they came!

BARBECUED ROAST IN FOIL
4-5 pound rolled roast

2 onions sliced thin	1 tablespoon prepared mustard
3 carrots sliced	¼ cup soy sauce
2-3 tablespoons chopped celery	½ cup tomato sauce or purée
1 clove garlic crushed	1 teaspoon salt
2 tablespoons butter	1 teaspoon pepper

Saute the onion, carrots, celery and garlic in butter for 5 minutes.
Combine the mustard with the soy sauce, tomato sauce, salt and
pepper and add it to the cooked vegetables. Meanwhile brown the
beef (preferably a rolled rib roast) on all sides over the coals. Put
part of the vegetable sauce on a large sheet of heavy foil. Place the
meat in the center and cover with remaining sauce. Fold over the
foil, doubling it at edges to keep juices in. Cook over low coals, turning several times, or cook on a spit for 1-1½ hours.   *Serves 8.*

STEW ON THE RANGE

Most traditional of all items of chuck in the cow country West was a beef stew of many ingredients and almost as many names. A few oldtimers, if they have the makin's handy, will still cook up a batch of "son-of-a-gun" at the drop of a howdy. These days, having the makin's handy is not always easy, for the prime requirement is a freshly killed beef, preferably a young one and "mighty fat"—even better if it wears someone else's brand.

Even in Texas there is not now and never has been a concensus on exactly how to slap together a son-of-a-gun. To set down a specific recipe as the exclusive gospel of cowcamp cookery would be like saying that all horses are sorrel. Nevertheless, a fairly typical version of this traditional beef stew would be something like this:

Cut into bite-size pieces about a fourth of a beef liver, a third of a heart, a helping of peeled tongue, sweetbreads, as many pounds of sirloin steak and lean neck meat as optimism suggests, a handful of paunch fat, and all of the butchered animal's marrowgut. Brown these ingredients in beef tallow in a cast iron Dutch oven. Add salt and a middling modicum of black pepper, barely cover with hot water, and simmer slowly for five or six hours. Stir and add water often enough to prevent sticking, but never soup it up thin. When almost done, add brains that have been browned separately. If the stew is cooked long and slowly enough it should have developed a creamy consistency without flour or other thickening—except maybe a few campfire ashes.

Choice of ingredients may vary considerably—except for one item. Without marrowgut, your stew is not bona fide son-of-a-gun. You may not find "marrowgut" in your dictionary, but it is easy to find inside a beef. It is the first few feet of the small intestine after it leaves the stomach. It contains a viscous, milky looking fluid which some people think is the last milk the calf swallowed—even if it's a two-year-old. Actually it is a natural secretion of the pancreas. Oldtimers are agreed that the marrowgut should not be washed out, merely cleaned on the outside before slicing. *This* is the magic ingredient that gives son-of-a-gun its special flavor.

What gives this concoction of "beef giblets" its many names is something else again. It is not hard to perceive that "son-of-a-gun" is a polite-company version of the original cowcamp name, nor that "rascal" would be another mild synonym. Nobody seems to know who first bestowed that original lilting, lusty designation which rhymes with "witch." Maybe some cranky chuckwagon cook so tagged it because he thought it was such a so-and-so to prepare.

In any case, from the derogatory nature of that original name there came many others, each indicating some person or character rated low in cowboy esteem. One favorite was "district attorney." Others were "banker," "governor," "high sheriff," and "brand inspector." Cowboys on the high plains called it "gentleman from Odessa," while buckaroos in the Odessa area were likely to term it "gentleman from Amarillo" or "Lovington." New Mexico cowboys sometimes just made a generality of it and called it "gentleman from Texas." Often the naming was more personal.

"Light and eat!" A wagonboss would thus invite a passerby. "We've got a nice batch of ol' Tom Todwinkle cooked up." The name used would be that of some well known grouch, bore or other unpopular character.

Such naming was not, of course, dead serious. This traditional make-believe of eating-an-enemy-by-proxy seems always to have been half the fun of enjoying a son-of-a-gun—just a bit of the free-and-easy cowboy humor that still survives, particularly in the southwestern cattle country.

Oddly enough, on some northwestern ranges "son-of-a-gun-in-a-sack" is a suet pudding dessert, hardly even a distant cousin of the son-of-a-you-know-what of longtime tradition.

A bold buckarooster called Mac,
Who wanted a wife in his shack,
Said: "Never mind looks!
I want one who cooks
Good son-of-a-gun-in-a-sack!"

RANCHER'S BEEF STEW

2 pounds lean stew beef cut into 1-inch cubes

2 tablespoons butter
1 onion chopped
Flour
1 cup consommé or 2 bouillon cubes
½ teaspoon salt
¼ teaspoon pepper

½ teaspoon savory
Pinch orégano
1 teaspoon Worcestershire sauce
1 teaspoon prepared mustard
Juice of ½ lemon
½ teaspoon minced parsley

Sauté the onion in butter. Dust beef pieces with flour, add to onion and brown thoroughly. Stir in the broth or 1 cup water and the bouillon cubes. Season with salt, pepper, savory and orégano. Simmer for about an hour until the meat is tender. Add Worcestershire, mustard and lemon juice and cook 10 minutes more. Add parsley and serve. *Serves 4.*

BEEF STEW

2½ pounds beef rump or chuck cut into 1-inch cubes

3 tablespoons bacon drippings, beef fat or oil
3 tablespoons flour
1 teaspoon salt
¼ teaspoon pepper
1 clove garlic crushed
1 bay leaf

3 tablespoons wine or 2 tablespoons wine vinegar
1 cinnamon stick
3 tablespoons tomato purée or 2 tablespoons tomato paste
1 pound small white onions (optional)

Brown the meat on all sides in the fat or oil; then sprinkle with flour, which has been mixed with the salt and pepper. Stir and brown the flour before adding ½ cup water and the rest of the ingredients, except onions. Add a little more water, if necessary, almost to cover the meat. Cover and simmer about 1½ hours, add the onions if you wish and simmer 20 to 30 minutes until they are tender. If the gravy is too thick, add a little water. Adjust seasoning to taste. Serve with vegetables and the gravy. *Serves 6.*

BEEF STEW WITH VEGETABLES

2½ pounds lean beef

2 tablespoons butter or
  olive oil
1 cup chopped onion
½ cup diced green peppers
½ cup diced celery
1 cup diced squash
1 cup cubed potatoes (white
  or sweet)

1 cup sliced carrots
1 cup canned or frozen
  corn
1½ teaspoons salt
¼ teaspoon pepper
2 tablespoons minced par-
  sley

Have the meat cut into 1-inch cubes and brown it in butter or oil. Add the onion, green peppers and celery and brown all together. Put into a kettle with 2 cups of water, the vegetables and salt and pepper. Cover and simmer for 1½ hours. Add a little water if needed and continue to cook unless the meat is tender. Adjust seasoning and sprinkle with parsley. The gravy should be thick enough.

Serves 6.

BEEF STEW IN RED WINE

(Boeuf Bourguignonne)

3½ to 4 pounds lean stew beef (sirloin, chuck, rump,
tip or round) cut into 1½-inch cubes

8 slices bacon or salt pork
1½ teaspoons salt
¼ teaspoon pepper
  Flour
1 onion sliced thin
1 carrot sliced thin
2 tablespoons chopped parsley

2 to 3 cups red wine
  Stock or water
½ teaspoon thyme
1 small bay leaf
¾ pound small white onions
1 pound mushrooms

Cut the bacon or salt pork into small pieces and brown in a Dutch oven or deep casserole. Remove the bacon or pork pieces and set aside. Season the meat with salt and pepper, and roll in a little flour. Brown the beef, a few pieces at a time, in the fat. Brown the sliced onion and carrot. Return meat to vegetables in the pot or casserole and add the parsley, wine and enough stock or water almost to cover the meat. Simmer in the oven or on top of the stove. When the meat is tender (about 2 hours), add the bacon or pork pieces and the onions, which have been browned in butter or bacon fat. Cook 15 minutes. Add the mushrooms, also sautéed, and cook an additional 10 to 15 minutes. Adjust seasoning and add a little thickening to the sauce if necessary.

Serves 8.

BEEF STEW WITH RICE AND CHEESE

3 pounds lean stew beef cut into 2½-inch pieces

½ pound bacon sliced thick or in one piece
1 cup thinly sliced onion
2 cups beef broth
1 cup vermouth
1 teaspoon salt
¼ teaspoon pepper
1 clove garlic crushed
1 bay leaf crushed
1 cup rice
2 tablespoons butter or oil
1½ cups canned tomatoes or 1 pound peeled and seeded fresh tomatoes
¾ cup grated cheese

Cut the bacon into cubes and fry until dry but not brown. Remove bacon bits to a casserole. Brown the meat quickly on all sides in the bacon drippings. Transfer pieces of meat to the casserole as you brown them. Sauté the onion for 2 minutes in the same skillet and add to the casserole. Add the broth and vermouth to the skillet, heat and pour over the meat. Add salt, pepper, garlic and bay leaf. Cover and simmer for about an hour until the meat is almost tender. Meanwhile, sauté the rice in oil or butter. Add tomatoes to the meat and cook half an hour. Stir in the rice and, if needed, a little more broth or water; the liquid should almost cover the stew. Cover and simmer 20 minutes without stirring. When finished, gently stir in the cheese. *Serves 6.*

WESTERN BEEF STEW

2 pounds stew beef (chuck or round) diced

3 tablespoons lemon juice
1½ teaspoons salt
¼ teaspoon pepper
2 teaspoons chili powder
⅓ cup flour
2 tablespoons oil
2 bouillon cubes
1 cup pitted ripe olives
2 tablespoons minced parsley

Sprinkle the beef with lemon juice and let stand for 2 hours, stirring a few times. Mix the salt, pepper and chili powder with the flour. Roll the meat in the seasoned flour until all sides are coated. Brown in oil. Add boiling water to cover and the bouillon cubes. Cover and simmer for 1½ hours until the meat is tender. Add the olives and heat 10 minutes. If the liquid is not thick enough, add remaining seasoned flour. Sprinkle with parsley before serving. *Serves 6.*

BEEF WITH SAUERKRAUT

1½ to 2 pounds beef cut into 1-inch cubes
2 onions chopped
2 tablespoons butter
1 teaspoon salt
¼ teaspoon pepper

½ teaspoon paprika
1 clove garlic crushed
1 pound sauerkraut

Brown the beef and onions in butter. Season with salt, pepper and paprika. Add the garlic, cover and simmer for half an hour. Add the sauerkraut and stir and cook for 15 minutes. Add ½ to ¾ cup water, cover and simmer for about an hour.   *Serves 4.*

A lassie from Kalamazoo
Attended a ranch barbecue.
She ate a whole lot
But never learned what
They put in the Western Beef Stew.

SPANISH RED WINE STEW

2½ pounds stew beef cut into 1-inch cubes
1 large onion sliced
2 tablespoons shortening or oil
1 clove garlic cut in half
1 (6 ounce) can tomato paste
1 cup red wine
1 teaspoon salt
¼ teaspoon pepper

¼ teaspoon paprika
1 tablespoon minced parsley
1 tablespoon minced chervil
1 tablespoon minced chives
12 new potatoes
Sausage or smoked ham (optional)

Fry the onion in shortening with the garlic. When the onion is light brown, remove the garlic and brown the meat, a few pieces at a time. Transfer meat and onion to a casserole. Add the tomato paste, mixed with an equal quantity of water, the wine, salt, pepper and herbs. Cover and simmer for about 45 minutes. Add the new potatoes and a few pieces of garlic sausage or smoked ham if you wish. If the liquid level is low, add more wine or water. Cover and simmer until the potatoes are done, about 25 minutes.   *Serves 6.*

FRENCH RED WINE BEEF CASSEROLE

2½ pounds lean stew beef cut into 1½-inch pieces

2 cups red wine	¼ teaspoon pepper
½ cup beef stock	½ pound mushrooms sliced
1 large onion sliced thin	(optional)
2 tablespoons butter	¾ pound small white onions
1 tablespoon flour	parboiled or 1 can
1 teaspoon salt	

Soak the beef in the red wine for 6 hours. Sauté the sliced onion in the butter until light brown. Brown the meat on all sides. Remove the meat and onion to a baking dish. Add flour to the drippings. Stir until brown and smooth; then add the broth and the wine in which the beef was marinated. Season with the salt and pepper and pour over the meat and onion. Cover and simmer until tender, about 1½ hours. Serve with or without the mushrooms, which have been sautéed in 2 tablespoons additional butter and added to the casserole just before serving. *Serves 6.*

GERMAN BEEF AND SAUERKRAUT STEW

2½ pounds round steak cut into 1-inch cubes

¼ cup butter	2 pounds sauerkraut
3 tablespoons paprika	2 teaspoons caraway seed
1 teaspoon salt	2 cups sour cream
2 cups chopped onion	

Brown the beef in the butter. Sprinkle with paprika and salt. Add the onion and sauté until brown. Put in the sauerkraut, cover tight and simmer for 1½ hours. Add a little water if necessary. Add the caraway seed during the last half hour of cooking. Just before serving, add the sour cream and stir until just heated through. *Serves 6.*

Buttermilk Smith was a real character, a Texas-New Mexico cowboy of the high plains. He was a lusty, leathery, rawhide, rollicky individual with his share of the dry wit.

Back in Territorial days, Buttermilk and several fellow cowpunchers found themselves with their hobbles off in Portales, New Mexico on a mighty dull Sunday: saloons closed, no movies, no dance, and mighty little whittlin'. They did find a restaurant which served steaks that weren't "all taller and no taste," and beans that "didn't rattle in the plate." That helped some, but not enough.

While they scalded their "goozlums" with a last round of coffee, the friendly cook in the hash house told them there was a revival meeting going on up the street, and he was sure they'd be welcome.

The preacher, earnest and sincere, had already worked up a pretty good sweat. He had "a hawg-callin' voice," a blackboard with figures on it, and a yardstick to point with.

"My friends," he intoned, "do you realize that in the past year the people of New Mexico have spent less than one hundred thousand dollars on education? And that they have spent only a measly fifty thousand on churches?" He paused. "While in the same period," he thundered, "they have spent over two hundred thousand dollars on whiskey and other strong drink?"

Suddenly Buttermilk Smith spoke up, loud and clear: "Yes, *sir!*" he declared. "And by jingo, parson, it was worth it!"

BEEF WITH BOURBON

2½ pounds beef round cut into cubes

2 tablespoons beef fat	1 teaspoon salt
1 onion minced	¼ teaspoon pepper
1 carrot diced	2 tablespoons meat glaze
½ cup consommé and ¼ cup white wine or ¾ cup consommé	⅓ cup bourbon
	2 tablespoons chopped parsley
2 tablespoons tomato purée	

Brown the beef in the fat and remove to a casserole. Brown the onion and carrot in the same fat and add this with the consommé to the beef. Add the wine, tomato purée, salt and pepper. Cover and cook in the oven for 1½ to 2 hours until the meat is tender. Add the meat glaze and bourbon and cook 15 minutes more. Adjust seasoning. Sprinkle with parsley and serve. Thicken the gravy with a little flour and water paste if you wish. *Serves 6.*

STEAK STEW WITH BRANDY

2 to 2½ pounds sliced fillet or boneless sirloin steak

2 tablespoons butter	1 teaspoon salt
¼ cup brandy	¼ teaspoon pepper
½ pound mushrooms sliced	¼ teaspoon paprika
½ cup beef or chicken broth	1 egg (optional)
½ (6 ounce) can tomato paste	¼ cup cream (optional)

Brown the fillet quickly in hot butter. Pour in 2 tablespoons warmed brandy and ignite. Add the mushrooms and, after a minute or two, the broth mixed with tomato paste. Season with salt, pepper and paprika. Simmer 5 minutes until the beef is tender but still rare inside. Heat remaining brandy and stir in. You may add 1 egg yolk, mixed with ¼ cup cream, just before serving if you wish.   *Serves 6.*

BEEF STEW WITH COFFEE

3 pounds chuck cut into 1-inch cubes

¼ cup flour	1 to 2 cups strong coffee
2 teaspoons salt	6 potatoes quartered
¼ teaspoon pepper	10 small white onions
2 tablespoons oil	4 carrots quartered length-
	wise

Mix the flour with salt and pepper and roll the meat in it. Brown the beef in oil. Add 1 cup coffee, cover and simmer for 1½ hours. Add the vegetables and cook another 30 to 40 minutes. Add more coffee if more liquid is needed. Thicken gravy with remaining seasoned flour.   *Serves 6.*

CHUCK WAGON STEW

3½ pounds chuck or rump cubed

1½ teaspoons meat tenderizer	3 potatoes peeled and
1 teaspoon salt	cubed
¼ teaspoon pepper	3 carrots sliced
2 tablespoons flour	8 small white onions
2 tablespoons oil	2 stalks celery sliced
1½ cups broth	

Sprinkle the meat tenderizer on all sides of the meat. Pierce the meat with a fork and let stand for half an hour at room temperature. If you use seasoned tenderizer, omit the salt. Roll the meat in seasoned flour and brown in the oil. Add the broth, cover and simmer for 1½ hours. Add the vegetables and cook another 20 minutes. Adjust seasoning.   *Serves 6-8.*

Potluck Pete, since he's been wed,
Claims he's been so darned well fed
On good beef stew by his new bride
That love has got him stew-pified!

BEEF AND KIDNEY STEW

2½ pounds lean stewing beef cut into 1½-inch cubes

2 beef kidneys	1 tablespoon Worcestershire
Flour	sauce
3 teaspoons salt	½ bay leaf crushed
½ teaspoon pepper	⅛ teaspoon thyme
3 to 4 tablespoons shortening	3 large onions minced
or salad oil	½ cup finely minced celery
2 tablespoons paprika	¼ cup minced parsley
1 tablespoon meat paste	1 clove garlic crushed
	½ pound mushrooms sliced

Remove the fat and sinews from the kidneys and slice them thin. Dredge the beef with flour. Season with 2 teaspoons salt and ¼ teaspoon pepper. Brown the beef well in the hot shortening or oil in a heavy kettle. Meanwhile, cover the kidneys with water, add 1 teaspoon salt and cook 15 to 20 minutes. Skim. Drain kidneys and strain the broth. Add enough water to the broth to make 1 quart and add to the browned beef. Season with ¼ teaspoon pepper and add the remaining ingredients, except the mushrooms. Cover and simmer about 2 hours over low heat. Add the sliced kidneys and mushrooms and cook about half an hour. Skim off fat and taste for seasoning. Thicken slightly with 2 tablespoons flour, mixed with a little cold water. Cook and stir a few minutes until the gravy is smooth and thickened. *Serves 6.*

GOULASH

2½ pounds lean beef cut into ¾-inch cubes

½ pound onions minced	2 teaspoons caraway seed
¼ cup lard, oil or butter	1 clove garlic
1 teaspoon salt	Broth or water
½ pound potatoes	

Fry the onion in the lard, oil or butter. Add the meat, salt and ¼ cup water. Cover and simmer for half an hour. Add a little more water or stock if needed. Peel and cut the potatoes into ¾ inch cubes. Add to the meat with the caraway, garlic and enough broth or water almost to cover. Simmer about 15 minutes until the potatoes are done. *Serves 6.*

ONION GOULASH

1½ pounds beef diced

1½ pounds onions chopped
fine

2 tablespoons shortening or
beef fat

1 tablespoon flour
1 teaspoon salt
½ teaspoon pepper
2 teaspoons paprika

Sauté the onions in the shortening. Season the meat with flour, which has been mixed with salt, pepper and paprika. Brown this with onions. Add about ½ cup of water, cover tight and simmer until the meat is tender. Add a little water if needed.   *Serves 4.*

HUNGARIAN GULYAS

2 pounds beef brisket cut into cubes

3 tablespoons oil
½ pound onions chopped
1 teaspoon salt
1 tablespoon paprika

1 pound potatoes cubed
1 tomato peeled and sliced
⅔ cup flour
1 egg

Put the beef into a saucepan with the onions. Add ¾ teaspoon salt and cook in the oil for 3 to 5 minutes. Add 2 cups of water and simmer until the meat is almost tender. Add the potatoes and more water if needed. Simmer again for 15 minutes. Add the tomato and cook only a few minutes. Mix the flour and egg, add a pinch of salt and roll out thin. Cut into small squares and boil in the stew for 2 to 3 minutes.   *Serves 6.*

GOULASH WITH SAUERKRAUT

2 pounds beef chuck cut in 1-inch cubes

3 onions sliced
3 tablespoons lard or beef fat
1 clove garlic
1 teaspoon paprika
1 teaspoon salt

1 teaspoon caraway seed
1 pound sauerkraut
⅓ cup rice
Sour cream

Brown the onions in fat. Add the meat and, after 2 minutes, the garlic, paprika, salt and caraway. Add 1 cup water, cover and simmer. As the water level goes down, add a little at a time. After half an hour, add the washed sauerkraut and more water. Cook until the meat is almost tender. Then add the rice, cover and cook 20 minutes. Fold in the sour cream just before serving.   *Serves 6.*

GOULASH WITH PEPPERS

3 pounds beef chuck or rump cut into 1½-inch pieces

2 slices bacon cut up
4 onions chopped
2 to 3 tablespoons paprika
1 teaspoon salt

¼ teaspoon pepper
2 to 3 large green peppers cut up
Flour (optional)

Brown the beef in a little beef fat and transfer to a large kettle. Add 1 cup water and simmer. Sauté the bacon and fry the onions in the bacon fat. Add the onions, bacon and drippings to the beef. Season with paprika, salt and pepper. Cover and simmer 1½ to 2 hours until the meat is tender. Add the peppers for the last half hour of cooking. Thicken the gravy with a little flour paste if you wish. *Serves 6.*

Beef for the grown-up! You can't go wrong!
Beef for pastor, beef for parishioner!
Beef for the kids! It keeps them strong—
Nature's own best heir conditioner!

BEEF STROGANOFF

1½ pounds boneless sirloin

¼ cup flour
1½ teaspoons salt
¼ teaspoon pepper
2 medium onions chopped fine
¼ cup butter
½ pound mushrooms sliced

1 clove garlic crushed
1 (10½ ounce) can consommé
1 pint sour cream
1 teaspoon paprika
1 tablespoon Worcestershire sauce

Cut the beef into pencil strips about 3 inches long. Dredge lightly with 2 tablespoons flour and season with 1 teaspoon salt and ¼ teaspoon pepper. Sauté the onions in the butter for 3 minutes. Add the mushrooms, garlic and the beef. Have the heat on high and toss the meat continuously. Cook 2 minutes—no more! Remove meat and vegetables. In the same pan add the remaining flour and blend. Add consommé and cook and stir until smooth. Add the sour cream, paprika, Worcestershire sauce and remaining salt and pepper. Keep the heat very low. When warm, add the beef-mushroom mixture and reheat. Adjust seasoning. *Serves 4.*

STROGANOFF WITH MUSHROOMS AND SHERRY

2 pounds sirloin cut into ½-inch strips

½ teaspoon salt	1 clove garlic crushed
¼ cup flour	2 tablespoons tomato paste
¼ cup butter	1 cup consommé or stock
1 pound mushrooms sliced	2 cups sour cream
¾ cup minced onion	¼ cup sherry

Mix the salt with 1 tablespoon flour and roll the beef in the mixture. Brown the beef quickly in 2 tablespoons very hot butter. Add the mushrooms, onion and garlic. Cook 3 to 4 minutes. Heat the remaining butter in a separate pan. Blend in the remaining flour. When smooth, add the tomato paste and consommé. Cook and stir until smooth. Pour over the beef. Stir in the sour cream and sherry and heat without boiling. *Serves 6.*

EASY BEEF STROGANOFF

1½ pounds beef fillet, sirloin or porterhouse

Flour	½ teaspoon salt
2 tablespoons butter	¼ teaspoon paprika
1 medium onion minced	¼ teaspoon basil or marjoram
½ pound mushrooms	½ to 1 cup sour cream

Cut the meat into fingersize pieces about 2 inches long. Sprinkle very lightly with flour and sauté in butter with the onion for 5 minutes. Add the mushrooms, salt, paprika, and basil or marjoram. Cook another 3 to 4 minutes. Add the sour cream and heat thoroughly. Adjust seasoning. *Serves 4.*

ECONOMY BEEF STROGANOFF

Use the recipe for Easy Beef Stroganoff° but substitute boneless lean round or chuck for the sirloin. Sprinkle generously with unseasoned meat tenderizer. Prick the meat with a fork to allow the tenderizer to penetrate. Set aside for half an hour. Then proceed as for Easy Beef Stroganoff.

It must be admitted that cowboys and Indians don't know about curry. That delicious seasoning was invented by an entirely different kind of Indian who lived in India possibly all of 5,000 years ago.

Curry powder as we know it today is a blend of fifteen to seventeen spices, including cardamom, poppy seed, mustard seed, ginger, coriander, turmeric, cloves, and so on. In India, curry powder is blended afresh by each cook each day. A visitor to India is given a different curry by each hostess. Here we make do with imported brands, or buy curry compounded in America by a known maker. Buy in small quantities, since curry loses its flavor by standing, especially in the light.

Curry is always accompanied on the table by a flotilla of little dishes, from which each diner help himself to chutney and several other condiments. Besides the inevitable chutney, the dishes may contain several items from the following list:

Shredded coconut
Ground peanuts or other nuts
Grated hard-boiled egg—
    usually yolk and white in separate dishes
Minced chives, scallions or onions
Chopped apple
Steamed raisins
Sliced or sautéed bananas
Sectioned oranges
Crumbled crisp bacon or chopped ham
India relish
Chopped crystallized or fresh ginger

BEEF CURRY

2 to 2½ pounds top round or top sirloin cut in bite-size pieces

½ cup flour
1 tablespoon curry powder
¼ cup butter
1 to 2 cloves garlic crushed
    or minced
½ cup raisins

1 cooking apple peeled,
    cored and chopped
½ cup chopped onion
¾ teaspoon salt
¼ teaspoon pepper
1 pound mushrooms sliced
    and sautéed in butter

Mix the flour with 2 teaspoons curry. Dredge the meat thoroughly and shake it a little in a wire sieve so that not too much flour clings. Melt the butter in a deep skillet or Dutch oven and add the garlic and meat, stirring often. When the meat is all browned, add 2 cups water, the raisins, apple and onion. Cover, lower heat and cook for 30 to 45 minutes until the meat is tender. Do not overcook. Season to taste with salt and pepper, and remaining curry. Add the mushrooms and remove from heat. The curry can be reheated on top of the range or in the oven. Serve with rice and condiments. *Serves 6.*

FRUITED BEEF CURRY

2½ pounds beef round or rump cut into 1-inch cubes

2 tablespoons curry powder

⅓ cup flour

1 stalk celery chopped

1 onion chopped

¼ cup butter

2 cup consommé or 2 bouillon cubes

1 teaspoon salt

½ teaspoon pepper

1 cup white seedless raisins

2 apples peeled, cored and diced

2 seedless oranges sectioned

1 banana sliced

Mix the curry with the flour and roll the meat lightly in the mixture. Brown the meat, celery and onion in the butter. Add the consommé, or 2 cups water and the bouillon cubes. Sprinkle with salt and pepper. Simmer until the meat is tender; the time will vary from 20 minutes to 1 hour, depending upon the cut of beef used. Don't overcook. Add the remaining ingredients and cook for 5 to 10 minutes. If the curry is not as thick as you wish, thicken with the leftover curry-flour mixture, blended with a little water. Adjust seasoning, adding more curry to taste. Serve with rice and condiments. *Serves 6.*

BEEF CURRY WITH BANANA

1½ to 2 pounds lean beef

2 tablespoons fat

½ cup chopped onion

2 teaspoons curry powder

½ cup chopped celery

1 teaspoon salt

¼ teaspoon paprika

¼ teaspoon pepper

2 tablespoons flour

1 large ripe banana sliced

1 egg

Trim the meat and cut into 1-inch cubes. Brown in the fat with the onion. Add 1 cup hot water, 1 teaspoon curry, celery, salt, pepper and paprika. Cover and simmer until tender, about ¾ hour. Mix remaining curry with the flour. Add the banana and stir into the meat. Simmer 10 minutes. Adjust seasoning to taste. Just before serving, mix the egg with 2 tablespoons water and stir into the curry. This should give a slightly cloudy streaked effect. Serve with rice and chutney and a selection of other condiments. *Serves 4.*

In the days of the open range, possessing plenty of beef on the hoof meant wealth, and not a few cowboys who acquired it got their start with a rope and a hot iron. Any unbranded bovine too mature to be following a branded cow was a maverick, and it was considered legitimate for anybody to slap his own brand on it. The "long ropers" also acquired cattle by altering brands. A rancher who found his I C brand changed to I C U by some poker-minded rustler promptly reclaimed the critter with I C U 2. B 4 got fixed over to B 4 U, and finally wound up as B 4 U 2. One rustler even seemed to confess his own rangeland rating by elongating S O to S O B, but the new brand he registered, once he had accumulated enough cattle to be respectable, was M I O, Spanish for "mine."

In these scientific days, nose-printing cattle can serve the same purpose of identification as finger-printing people. But it takes a heap more ink!

Warning to rustlers: Leave those mavericks alone, and stay out of the jailhouse!

BURMESE BEEF CURRY

2½ pounds sirloin cut into 1-inch strips

3 tablespoons peanut oil
2 medium onions chopped
1 clove garlic crushed
1 tablespoon chopped fresh
    ginger or 1 teaspoon
    powdered

1 teaspoon salt
Pinch powdered saffron
¼ teaspoon chili powder
2 teaspoons curry powder
2 tablespoons soy sauce

Heat the oil. Add the onions, garlic, ginger, salt, saffron and chili powder. Add the meat and cook until browned. Add 1 cup water or beef stock and the curry, blended with the soy sauce. Cover and simmer 20 to 30 minutes. Serve with rice, with or without condiments. *Serves 6.*

JAIL HOUSE CHILI

2 pounds bottom round diced

1 large onion chopped
2 tablespoons shortening or
    bacon drippings
2 tablespoons flour
2 cloves garlic minced
1 teaspoon oregano

¼ teaspoon ground cumin or
    1 teaspoon cumin seed
1 tablespoon chili powder
2 teaspoons salt
3 to 4 (1 pound 4 ounce)
    cans kidney beans

Brown the onion and beef in the shortening or bacon drippings. Stir in the flour, cook 2 minutes and add all the remaining ingredients, except beans. Simmer for about half an hour, add beans and simmer until the beef is tender. Adjust seasoning. *Serves 8.*

BEEF WITH OLIVES

3 pounds lean stew beef cut into 1½-inch cubes

2 tablespoons butter or oil	¼ teaspoon pepper
2 cups broth	½ cup raisins (optional)
1 teaspoon salt	30 small stuffed olives

Brown the meat in butter or oil. Put into a kettle with all of the other ingredients. Cover and simmer about 1½ hours until the beef is tender. Thicken juices with a little flour if you wish. *Serves 6.*

HERBED BEEF CASSEROLE

2 pounds round or chuck cut into 1½-inch cubes

2 tablespoons butter	¼ teaspoon pepper
½ pound small white onions	¼ teaspoon marjoram
½ pound mushrooms	¼ teaspoon rosemary
1 teaspoon tomato paste	¼ teaspoon thyme
3 tablespoons flour	1 bay leaf
1 cup broth	2 tablespoons minced
½ cup red wine	parsley
1 teaspoon salt	

Brown the beef in butter. Remove to a casserole. Brown the onions. Add the mushrooms, cut in half if they are large, and sauté 2 minutes. Pour over the meat. Put the tomato paste and flour into the pan and stir until smooth. Add the broth and cook 3 minutes. Pour over the meat and add the wine, salt, pepper and herbs. Bake, covered, in a 350° oven for 2 hours. Add a little more wine if needed.
Serves 6.

DICE OF BOILED BEEF

3 pounds beef cut out in 1-inch cubes

1 tablespoon salt	3 to 4 carrots cut up
Few peppercorns	3 onions quartered
1 bay leaf	3 stalks celery cut into ½-
¼ teaspoon monosodium	inch sticks
glutamate	3 potatoes quartered

Put the beef in a pot and cover with water. Bring to a boil with the salt, peppercorns, bay leaf and monosodium glutamate. Simmer for about half an hour until soft but not thoroughly done. Add carrots, onions and celery and cook 15 minutes. Add the potatoes and cook another 15 minutes. Thicken the juices slightly with flour paste.
Serves 6.

There was nothing the cowman boss of the Circle O Guest Ranch liked better than succulent oxtail stew the way his wife prepared it.

"Now, Leander," she warned him one evening before calling in the guests for dinner, "I wouldn't want to say anything that might embarrass our guests, so if I frown at you during dinner, it means you are not to take a second helping of the oxtail stew. You are to stop eating right there."

"Glad you warned me, Sugar Woman," replied her husband with a grin. "I ain't much of a hand to talk at table, either, so if I frown right back at you, it means I ain't goin' to stop eatin' till I get good and ready!"

OXTAIL STEW

3 oxtails jointed

2 tablespoons oil or shortening
1 tablespoon dry mustard
1 tablespoon cornstarch
1 tablespoon chili powder
1 teaspoon salt
½ teaspoon pepper

Juice of 1 orange
Juice of ½ lemon
1 cup broth
1 large onion minced
½ cup diced celery
1 (4 ounce) jar pimientos
1 cup pitted olives (optional)

Brown the oxtails in oil. Mix the mustard, cornstarch, chili powder, salt and pepper with the orange and lemon juices, broth and 1 cup water. Add to the meat. Cover and simmer for about 2 hours. Add the onion, celery, pimientos and the olives if you wish. Simmer half an hour. Adjust seasoning and thicken juices if you wish with a little more cornstarch.   *Serves 4.*

OXTAIL RAGOUT

6 oxtails cut in 1½- to 2-inch pieces

3 tablespoons olive or salad
  oil
Flour
5 onions sliced
3 cloves garlic crushed
1 cup minced parsley
2 tablespoons minced fresh
  mint
1 teaspoon basil
1¼ teaspoons salt
¼ teaspoon pepper

¾ cup chopped seeded
  green peppers
¾ cup coarsely chopped carrots
½ cup consommé
½ cup dry red wine
1 (1 pound 14 ounce) can
  tomatoes
2 (8 ounce) cans tomato
  sauce

Heat the oil in a large Dutch oven. Lightly flour the oxtails and brown well in the hot oil and set them aside. Sauté the onions and garlic until golden brown. Season with the parsley, mint, basil, salt and pepper. Stir and cook 5 minutes longer. Add the green peppers, carrots, consommé and wine. Simmer 2 to 3 minutes and add the tomatoes and tomato sauce. Stir the sauce very well and return oxtails to the sauce. Cover tight and simmer for about 2 hours. Bake, covered, in a 300° oven for another 2 hours until the meat is quite tender. Skim well before serving. *Serves 8.*

BRAISED OXTAILS

4 oxtails

2 teaspoons salt	Parsley
¼ teaspoon pepper	2 bay leaves crushed
Flour	8 carrots cut in pieces
¼ cup shortening	16 small white onions
2 quarts consommé or 8 bouil-	2 (8 ounce) cans tomato
lon cubes and 2 quarts	sauce
water	2 tablespoons paprika
Celery leaves	

Have your butcher joint the oxtails. Dredge with salt, pepper and flour and brown in the shortening in a heavy pot with a lid. When the meat is well browned, add consommé or water and bouillon cubes, a handful or so of celery leaves, several sprigs of parsley and the bay leaves. Cover and simmer over very low heat about 2 hours, or put the pot in the oven for about 3 hours. Stir occasionally and add water if stock becomes too reduced. When meat is almost tender, add the carrots, whole onions, tomato sauce and paprika. Cook another half hour until vegetables are tender.
Serves 6.

For newlyweds there's naught can sweeten
The road ahead like happy eatin'.
He'll broil the steak, she'll cook the stew,
And roasts can be prepared by two.
On beef they'll sail through life a-whizzin',
If he likes hers and she likes hisn.

TEXAS CHILI

1½ pounds beef cut in small cubes

3 tablespoons shortening	1 teaspoon cumin seed
¾ cup chopped onion	2 teaspoons salt
1 clove garlic crushed	2 tablespoons flour
1 to 2 tablespoons chili powder	Red kidney beans

Brown the meat in the shortening. Add the onion and garlic and sauté for a few minutes. Stir in the chili powder, cumin seed, salt and 3 cups water. Cover and simmer about an hour until the meat is very tender. Thicken juices with the flour, mixed with ¼ cup water. Serve over kidney beans. *Serves 4 to 6.*

BARBECUED BEEF CASSEROLE

1½ pounds round steak cut into 1-inch cubes

2 tablespoons butter	2 tablespoons Worcester-
¼ teaspoon freshly ground pepper	shire sauce
12 small white onions	½ cup catchup
2 cloves garlic crushed	1 teaspoon salt
½ cup vinegar	2 teaspoons dry mustard
1 tablespoon brown sugar	2 cups cooked or canned peas

Heat the butter in a skillet and brown the meat. Sprinkle with pepper. Add ¼ cup water and the remaining ingredients, except the peas. Pour into a 2-quart casserole, cover and bake in a 325° oven for 1½ hours. Stir in the peas, cover and bake another 10 minutes. *Serves 4.*

THIS AND THAT

Neither the Indians of the West nor non-Indian, non Spanish pioneers had to learn from the Spaniards how to preserve red meat by sun-drying it. This was an ancient art they already knew about from their own ancestors—like they knew not to expectorate against a forty mile breeze. But it was from the language of the Spaniards that this durable delicacy derived the designation by which it has been known ever since, even unto the latest dictionary.

Charqui (pronounced CHAR-kee) the Spaniards called it. But we English speaking Americans never have been much inclined to fool around with foreign spellings and pronunciations. *Charqui* sounded enough like "jerky" to suit the early pioneers' ears, and the name has stuck—the same way jerky stuck to their ribs.

In a sunny season in the usually dry air of much of the West, making jerky was no great problem—still isn't, for that matter. Just cut lean beef, venison or other red meat in strips about as thin as a politician's promise and flip them over a clothesline to dry. Lacking clotheslines, Indians and frontiersmen hung their meat on whatever they had handy: ropes, stretched buckskin strips, willow withes, sticks, scrub oak brush—just so they got it out in the sun and fresh air. Meat spread out on rock formations with a tilt toward the sun would also dry in a hurry.

Strictly lean meat, stripped with the grain, worked best. Fat would go rancid. A little salt might hasten the curing, but it was neither essential nor often used. There may have been such comestible items as mutton and pork jerky, but if so, this writer never heard of them. Somehow the idea does not sound very appetizing.

Frontier jerky, properly dried, was almost hard enough to drive nails with—if there had been any nails to drive—and if kept dry, would keep practically forever. It could be stewed to an edible tenderness, but in the Old West untold tons of it were simply sliced off in thin shavings with a pocketknife and eaten raw. By carrying a few chunks of jerky in his pocket, a man could start chewing on it early in the morning and eat breakfast, noon-dinner and supper without ever getting off his horse—or mule, if his name happened to be Kit Carson.

Although reliance upon jerky as a staple ration dwindled away with the settling up of the West, it certainly did not entirely vanish with the stagecoach. Some old cowhands would still rather chew jerky than spearmint. I once asked Buttermilk Smith to describe its flavor.

"Well, sir," he told me, "first off, it's kinder like chawin' on a well weathered leather boot, but after while that good ol' meat flavor comes alive so rich and tangy that you purt near hate to lose it by swallerin'. It's kinder like eatin' salted peanuts or kissin' a purty gal: once you get started, you keep right on a-reachin' for more."

Pemmican, the standby C-ration of northwestern explorers, beaver trappers, *voyageurs,* and other frontiersmen, was jerky plus "fixin's." "Pemmikkan" is a Cree Indian word, and it was from the Indians that white men learned to prepare it. After pounding or stone-grinding thoroughly dried jerky practically into a powder, the expert pemmican makers would stuff a rawhide bag with it, then pour in heat-rendered fat, pack the whole mass down good and solid, then seal the bag as nearly airtight as possible with tallow. Such bags, which would stand all kinds of rough handling, were standard items of commerce among the trappers, *voyageurs* and fur companies of the Northwest.

When available, wild currants or even chokecherries were sometimes mixed with the pounded meat. While this might improve the flavor, it was the meat and tallow that counted when it came to filling hungry stomachs and keeping far-ranging outdoorsmen strong and healthy. While pemmican could be eaten uncooked in an emergency, it was less palatable that way than raw jerky.

Preparing pemmican after a buffalo kill was "big doin's." The Mountain Men called it "makin' meat."

CHIPPED BEEF IN CREAM
½ pound chipped beef

2 tablespoons minced onion	2 cups milk
1 tablespoon minced green pepper	1 tablespoon minced parsley
3 tablespoons butter	¼ teaspoon paprika
3 tablespoons flour	¼ teaspoon pepper
	3 tablespoons sherry (optional)

Sauté the onion and pepper in butter until light brown. Sprinkle with the flour and add the milk slowly while stirring. Add the beef, which has been pulled apart, and simmer until thickened. Just before serving, add the parsley, paprika, pepper, and the sherry if you wish. Good served on toast. *Serves 4.*

CHIPPED BEEF IN CHEESE SAUCE
½ pound chipped beef

2 tablespoons butter	1 cup grated or finely diced cheese
2 tablespoons flour	
1½ cups milk	½ teaspoon prepared mustard
⅛ teaspoon paprika	

Melt the butter, stir in the flour and blend. Add the milk slowly while stirring. When the sauce is smooth, add the cheese, paprika and beef and stir gently. Season with mustard. Serve on toast, English muffins or hot corn bread if you wish. *Serves 4.*

Steers fattened on corn are said to be "corned,"
So, asking for "corned beef," you'd better be warned
To specify carefully, make it quite clear,
Or you might get short ribs from a corn-fattened steer!

CHIPPED BEEF CREOLE
4-5 ounces chipped beef

¼ cup minced onion	2 tablespoons butter
¼ cup minced celery	1 (10 ounce) can tomato soup
2 tablespoons minced green pepper	Toast, rice or noodles (optional)
1 tablespoon minced parsley	

Cut or pull the beef into large shreds. Sauté the vegetables in butter until soft, but not brown, about 5 minutes. Add the soup and bring to a boil. Stir in the beef and heat for 2 minutes. Serve on toast, rice or noodles if you wish. *Serves 4.*

CHIPPED BEEF ROLL-UPS

4 ounces chipped beef

3-4 ounces cream cheese
1-2 tablespoons cream
1 tablespoon horseradish

Watercress or parsley
(optional)

Have the cheese at room temperature. Soften with cream, blend in the horseradish. Spread on slices of chipped beef and roll up. If rolls tend to unroll, secure with toothpicks. Decorate ends with a sprig of watercress or parsley. *Serves 8 as canapés.*

Chipped beef is also called dried beef.

CORNED BEEF

3- to 4-pound piece brisket of corned beef

2 onions sliced
3 cloves
1 bay leaf
1 clove garlic cut up
1 stalk celery cut up

1 carrot cut in rounds
3 sprigs parsley
¼ teaspoon coarsely ground
pepper

Put the meat in a large kettle. Add all of the ingredients and cover with water. Cover, bring to a boil and then simmer for about 3 hours until the meat is tender. From time to time remove the scum as it appears on the top. Slice thin to serve. Good with cabbage cooked in the same water. *Serves 6 to 8.*

GLAZED CORNED BEEF

4-pound piece lean brisket of corned beef

Cloves
¾ cup brown sugar

½ teaspoon dry mustard
¼ cup sherry

Cover the beef with water and simmer until almost tender, about 3½ hours. Drain and place in a baking dish. Score the fat and stick with cloves. Mix the sugar, mustard and sherry and add a few tablespoons of the corned beef stock. Pour this over, cover and bake one-half to three-fourths hour in a 350° oven. Baste frequently. Serve hot or cold, sliced thin. *Serves 8.*

NEW ENGLAND CORNED BEEF DINNER

4- to 5-pound piece brisket of corned beef

1 teaspoon salt	8 small potatoes cut in half
¼ teaspoon pepper	or 4 to 6 larger ones
2 teaspoons sugar	quartered
1 clove garlic	6 carrots cut into 2-inch
1 bay leaf	pieces
6 red chili peppers (optional)	8 medium onions
8 small turnips cut in half	1 head cabbage

Put the meat in a deep pot, cover with water, and add the salt, pepper, sugar, garlic, bay leaf, and the chili peppers if available. Simmer until the meat is tender, about 3 hours. Add the turnips, potatoes, carrots and onions and cook 15 minutes. Then add the cabbage, cut into 6 or 8 wedges. Cover and cook 15 minutes more. Put the meat on a warmed platter and put the vegetables around. Spoon a little juice over all.   *Serves 8.*

CORNED BEEF HASH

2 pounds cooked corned beef chopped

4 boiled potatoes chopped	1 small onion grated
Salt	2 tablespoons butter
¼ teaspoon pepper	¼ cup cream

Mix the corned beef and freshly cooked potatoes. There should be twice as much corned beef as potatoes. Add salt to taste and the pepper and onion. Fry in butter in a very hot heavy skillet. Reduce heat and cook slowly, adding cream now and then to keep moist. Brown the top under broiler or turn out bottom-side-up on a platter.   *Serves 6.*

MARK HANNA HASH

1 pound corned beef

4 baked potatoes	1 teaspoon onion juice
2 tablespoons butter	Dash nutmeg
1 teaspoon salt	Chicken stock
¼ teaspoon pepper	

Scoop out freshly baked potatoes. Add an equal quantity of diced corned beef, which has been heated in the butter. Season with salt, pepper, onion juice and nutmeg. Add enough stock to moisten. Reheat in the potato shells. Dot top with a little additional butter if you wish.   *Serves 4.*

TOMATOES STUFFED WITH CORNED BEEF HASH

2 (1 pound) cans corned beef hash

8 to 10 tomatoes	2 tablespoons flour
1 teaspoon salt	1 cup milk
½ teaspoon onion salt	¼ teaspoon thyme
¼ teaspoon pepper	¼ teaspoon marjoram
2 tablespoons butter	¾ cup grated Cheddar cheese

Cut the tops off the tomatoes, scoop out the pulp and set aside. Mix the hash with ½ teaspoon salt, onion salt and ⅛ teaspoon pepper. Fill the tomatoes. Make a cream sauce with the butter, flour and milk. Season with ½ teaspoon salt, thyme, marjoram and a little pepper. When sauce is smooth, stir in the cheese until melted. Add ½ cup tomato pulp. Arrange the filled tomatoes in a casserole and pour the sauce around them. Bake in a 375° oven for about half an hour until the tomatoes are tender and heated through. Serve the sauce over the tops of the tomatoes. *Serves 8 to 10.*

Though San Francisco was doubtless tops for early day eateries in the West, several other boomtowns pretty well held their own, notably Denver and Central City, Colorado. Along with the latter's annual summer opera, its noted Teller House has revived old fame with "The Face On the Barroom Floor," a pretty brunette painted in 1936 by Herndon Davis.

Denver's claim to dining fame would seem to center on the Brown Palace Hotel. Since 1892 traditional host to the famous, including many Presidents of the United States, it may well be the only hotel in the world ever to entertain beef-on-the-hoof within its high-toned walls. When Dan Thorton, later state governor, got $50,000 each for two blue ribbon Hereford bulls, both critters were guests in corrals in the Brown Palace lobby for the duration of the 1945 Stock Show!

BLUE RIBBON SHORT RIBS

3 pounds short ribs

1 onion chopped	½ teaspoon curry
1 carrot sliced	1 clove garlic minced
4 stalks celery and leaves	(optional)
chopped	2 tablespoons flour
1 teaspoon salt	2 to 3 tablespoons sour
½ teaspoon pepper	cream (optional)

Have the ribs cut into serving pieces. Put into a kettle with a quart of water and the onion, carrot, celery, salt, pepper and curry; add the garlic if you wish. Cover and simmer until almost tender, 1 to 1½ hours. Heat oil in a heavy skillet and brown the meat on all sides. Skim fat from gravy and pour a cup of the gravy over the ribs. Cook, uncovered, in a 350° oven for half an hour. Add more gravy if needed. Meanwhile, thicken remaining gravy with flour. Stir in the sour cream if you wish and pour over the ribs.   *Serves 4 to 6.*

BAKED SHORT RIBS
3 pounds short ribs

2 teaspoons salt	3 tablespoons vinegar or
½ teaspoon pepper	lemon juice
½ teaspoon chili powder	1 clove garlic crushed
1 teaspoon sugar	1 large onion sliced
2 tablespoons oil	

Have the ribs cut into serving pieces. Mix all of the rest of the ingredients together and pour over the ribs in a deep bowl. Marinate in refrigerator for 12 to 24 hours, stirring a few times. Remove ribs and put into a roasting pan in a 450° oven for 20 minutes. Pour marinade, onions and all, over the ribs; cover and bake in 350° oven for an hour. Cook, uncovered, for 20 minutes longer to brown. Thicken juices slightly with flour if you wish and adjust seasoning to taste.   *Serves 4.*

BURGUNDY SHORT RIBS WITH VEGETABLES
5 pounds short ribs

3 tablespoons flour	¼ teaspoon marjoram
2 tablespoons bacon fat	1 carrot diced
1 cup (scant) chopped	1 cup Burgundy wine
onion	¾ cup beef broth
1½ teaspoons salt	6 medium potatoes
½ teaspoon pepper	6 small carrots
1 teaspoon sugar	12 small white onions

Have the ribs cut into serving pieces and roll them in flour. Brown on all sides in the fat. Add onion, salt, pepper, sugar, marjoram and diced carrot. Pour on ¾ cup wine and ½ cup water. Cover and simmer for an hour. Skim off excess fat, add broth and remaining wine and simmer for another half hour. Add potatoes, carrots and onions. Simmer, covered, until vegetables are tender, about 25 minutes. Thicken juices with remaining flour and adjust seasoning.   *Serves 6.*

BRAISED SHORT RIBS

6 to 7 pounds short ribs cut into serving-size pieces

2 teaspoons liquid smoke (optional)

1 teaspoon salt

½ cup plus 2 tablespoons flour

2 tablespoons shortening or salad oil

1 bay leaf crumbled

1 (10½ ounce) can consommé

If you wish, sprinkle the meat on all sides with liquid smoke, brushing it in with a pastry brush. Mix the salt with ½ cup flour. Dust the ribs with the flour (save any flour not used). Brown the meat in the shortening or oil in a large roaster or Dutch oven. Add the rest of the seasoned flour, stirring smoothly into the drippings in the pan. Crumble the bay leaf over the meat, add ¼ cup water, cover and simmer over low heat about 2½ hours until beef is tender. Lift short ribs, cool the meat slightly and remove bones. Drain off all but 2 tablespoons fat and blend in 2 tablespoons flour and the consommé. Cook and stir until smooth. Place beef back in gravy to heat. *Serves 8.*

BARBECUED SHORT RIBS

3 pounds short ribs cut into 2- to 3-inch pieces

2 tablespoons shortening or salad oil

1 medium onion chopped

3 tablespoons vinegar

2 tablespoons brown sugar

1 cup catchup

3 tablespoons Worcestershire sauce

1 teaspoon prepared mustard

½ cup diced celery

2 teaspoons salt

⅛ teaspoon pepper

1 tablespoon flour

Brown the ribs in shortening or oil. Add the onion and cook until browned. Put in ½ cup water and remaining ingredients, except the flour. Cover and simmer slowly about 1½ hours until tender; or bake, covered, in a 350° oven. Skim off the fat and thicken the juices with the flour blended with a little cold water. Good served with noodles or rice. *Serves 4.*

BOILED SHORT RIBS

4 pounds short ribs cut up

1 bay leaf

1 onion

2 teaspoons salt

5 peppercorns

Place the meat in a large kettle and cover with water. Add the remaining ingredients. Cover. Simmer over low heat for about 3½ hours until tender. Remove ribs and let the broth cool. Remove fat from the broth and reheat ribs and broth together. Good served with horseradish sauce. *Serves 6.*

If you are a girl, tall or petite,
And want to charm the men you meet,
When they invite you out to eat,
You'll order hash instead of meat.

Leftovers can be delicious. In fact, you may want to buy more beef than you need, to prepare a *planned* leftover dish such as Shepherd's Pie or Beef Hash. Try some of the following recipes and do some experimenting on your own.

LEFTOVER BEEF HASH

3 to 4 cups cubed leftover beef

1 onion chopped	1 teaspoon salt
¼ cup butter	⅛ teaspoon pepper
⅓ cup diced celery	3 tablespoons tomato paste
3 tablespoons chopped green pepper	½ cup leftover beef gravy or stock
1 cup cubed potato	

Sauté the onion in butter. Add the celery, green pepper and potato. Season with salt and pepper. Cook until potatoes are almost tender. Add the tomato paste, gravy or stock and the beef. Cover and simmer 10 minutes. *Serves 4 to 6.*

ROAST BEEF HASH

2½ cups diced leftover roast beef

2 cups diced cooked potatoes	¼ teaspoon pepper
1 tablespoon minced onion	¼ teaspoon paprika
1 teaspoon salt	2 tablespoons butter

Combine all of the ingredients in a skillet with the butter. Brown, turn with a spatula and brown the other side. You may form the hash into 4 patties for ease of turning over. Total cooking time is about 8 minutes. *Serves 4.*

ROAST BEEF HASH WITH EGGS

Use the recipe for Roast Beef Hash. After you have turned the 4 patties, make an indentation in each with a spoon. Drop an egg into each hollow, cover the pan and cook until the eggs are set; or cover and put into a 350° oven for about 10 minutes until the eggs are set. *Serves 4.*

BAKED ROAST BEEF HASH

3 cups diced cooked beef

2 tablespoons minced onion	Salt
3 tablespoons butter	Pepper
2 to 3 tablespoons flour	2 cups diced cooked potatoes
1 cup beef stock or leftover gravy or a combination	1 cup soft bread crumbs

Sauté the onion in 2 tablespoons butter. Blend in the flour, add stock and cook until smooth and blended. Add salt and pepper to taste. Gently stir in the meat and potatoes and put into a buttered casserole or baking pan. Top with bread crumbs and dot with butter. Bake in a 350° oven for half an hour. *Serves 4.*

LEFTOVER BEEF WITH APPLES

3 cups diced cooked beef

1 cup beef gravy or:	2 apples peeled and sliced
2 tablespoons butter	1 tablespoon sugar
2 tablespoons flour	Salt
1 cup beef consommé	

Simmer the apple slices 5 minutes in beef gravy, or make gravy by blending butter and flour in a skillet, add consommé slowly and cook 3 to 4 minutes. Add meat and sugar, and salt to taste. Serve as soon as heated through. *Serves 4.*

BEEF WITH RICE AND VEGETABLES

2 cups cooked beef cut in strips

½ pound mushrooms sliced or quartered	2 tablespoons soy sauce
¼ cup butter	2 cups cooked rice
½ green pepper diced	1 tomato peeled and diced (optional)
1 stalk celery sliced thin	Salt
1 large onion diced	2 eggs
1 clove garlic crushed	½ head lettuce chopped

Sauté the mushrooms in the butter for 2 minutes. Add the green pepper, celery, onion and garlic. Mix in the soy sauce, rice, beef, and the tomato if you wish. Heat through, stirring occasionally. It will brown a bit. Add salt to taste. Just before serving, break the raw eggs into the mixture and stir together quickly. Mix in the lettuce and serve at once so the lettuce will stay crisp and the eggs won't overcook.   *Serves 4 to 6.*

DEVILED GRILLED BEEF RIBS

6 cold cooked roast beef rib bones

3 tablespoons melted butter
2 tablespoons vinegar
Bread crumbs

Sauce

2 tablespoons butter
1 to 2 teaspoons prepared
   mustard

1 teaspoon tarragon vinegar
1 teaspoon Worcestershire
   sauce
½ teaspoon salt
¼ teaspoon pepper
1 egg yolk
Dash Tabasco sauce

Separate the ribs. Rub with melted butter to which the vinegar has been added. Roll in the bread crumbs. Grill until brown on both sides. Meanwhile, make the sauce by combining all the ingredients. Put about half the sauce on a hot platter, put the ribs on top and pour the remaining sauce over the ribs.   *Serves 4 to 6.*

Leftovers from beef are good eating, that's true,
Except that leftovers from *beef* are so few!

COLD CUBES OF BEEF

2 pounds cooked beef cut into 1-inch cubes

½ cup olive or salad oil
¼ cup vinegar
1 teaspoon dry mustard
½ teaspoon celery salt
1 teaspoon salt
¼ teaspoon pepper

2 onions chopped
2 tomatoes diced
¼ teaspoon orégano
1 teaspoon minced parsley
¼ teaspoon garlic powder
   (optional)

Put the meat in a marinade of the oil, vinegar, mustard, celery salt, salt and pepper. Let stand for at least an hour, turning the meat once or twice. Add the onions, tomatoes, orégano, parsley, and the garlic powder if you wish. Mix and let stand at least 15 minutes. Drain and serve cold on a bed of lettuce if you wish.

Serves 4.

LEFTOVER MEAT LOAF

2½ cups chopped cooked beef

2 tablespoons butter
1½ tablespoons flour
1 cup milk or half milk and half broth
½ teaspoon salt
⅛ teaspoon pepper
1 egg

⅓ cup fresh bread crumbs
1 tablespoon minced parsley
1 tablespoon minced onion
Mustard Sauce* or Tomato Sauce* (optional)

Melt the butter, add the flour and blend and cook several minutes. Add the milk, salt and pepper slowly while stirring. Cool the sauce and beat in the egg. Add the beef, bread crumbs, parsley and onion. Mix well. Form into a loaf and put into a greased baking dish. Bake in a 050° oven for 15 to 20 minutes. Serve with hot Mustard Sauce or Tomato Sauce if you wish. *Serves 4.*

SHEPHERD'S PIE I

3 cups chopped cooked beef

2 onions sliced thin
¼ cup butter or margarine
2 tablespoons flour
1½ cups beef broth or consommé
1 carrot minced

1 tablespoon minced parsley
¼ teaspoon pepper
Salt
1 pound potatoes mashed and seasoned

Sauté the onions in butter or margarine until browned. Add flour and brown. Add broth and cook and stir until smooth. Add the carrot, parsley and pepper. Simmer for 5 to 10 minutes. If too thick, add more broth or water. Add salt to taste; the quantity will depend upon the seasoning in the broth. Put the meat in a deep pie dish. Pour the sauce over. Cover the top with seasoned mashed potatoes. Bake in a 400° oven until heated through and potatoes browned on top. If all of the ingredients are very hot when the pie is put together, the browning of the top of the potatoes can be done under the broiler. *Serves 4.*

The good taste of beef is anchored inside it.
Try as you may, you simply can't hide it.
Meat balls and spaghetti? Meat loaf hot or hotter?
It's still that beef flavor that makes your mouth water!

SHEPHERD'S PIE II

3 cups chopped cooked beef

2 eggs
2 cups seasoned mashed
  potatoes
2 tablespoons minced par-
  sley
½ teaspoon salt
Butter

¼ cup cooked, chopped
  celery
⅓ cup cream or ½ cup
  tomato sauce
Grated cheese (optional)

Mix the beaten egg yolks with potatoes. Beat the whites until stiff and fold into the potatoes. Line a baking dish with half of the potato mixture. Mix the meat with the parsley, celery, cream or tomato sauce, and salt. Pour into the potato-lined baking dish. Spread remaining potato mixture over the top and dot with butter. Sprinkle with cheese if you wish. Bake in a 400° oven until the top is browned. *Serves 4.*

HUNTSMAN'S PIE

3 cups minced cooked beef

1 pound cooked potatoes
  sliced thin
2 onions sliced thin
2 apples peeled and sliced
  thin

1 teaspoon salt
¼ teaspoon pepper
1 cup broth
¼ cup bread crumbs
2 tablespoons butter

Make layers of potatoes, meat, onions and apples in a baking dish, ending with potatoes on top. Sprinkle with salt and pepper and pour the broth over. Sprinkle with bread crumbs and dot with butter. Bake in a 350° oven for about an hour. *Serves 4.*

Most cowpokes will tell you that here is a truth
You might as well learn in the days of your youth:
To be a cowpuncher you'll never learn how
Unless you are purt' near as smart as the cow!

SAUCE FOR THE BEEF

The cook a-cuttin' sirloin steak, the cowhands waitin' 'round,
So they got to kinder talkin' about the diff'rent things they'd found
That each of them was thankful for on this Thanksgiving Day,
And some they told it solemn-like, and some they told it gay.
Tom thanked the Lord that horses had four legs instead of two,
So cowboys didn't have to walk like some poor idiots do.
Ol' Bashful claimed that women was the blessing in his life—
No doubt he meant his mother, for he'll never git a wife!
"I'm thankful most for cattle, boys," said Slim, who thinks
    a heap.
"In a world without them critters we would all be herdin' sheep!"
The Ramrod spoke his thankfulness that grass was good and long,
And Curly said he thanked the Lord that he was young and
    strong.
Budinkus blessed his appetite. The way that beefsteak smelt,
He also felt thanksgivin' for the long holes in his belt.
Ol' Dunk, he kinder sucked his pipe and gazed out toward
    the hills.

"Well, boys," he says, "I'm sixty-five and full of liver pills.
My rheumatism aches me, and my pipe is gittin' stale.
My hossy days is over, and I'm feelin' purty pale.
I've got some nose for smellin' left—that beefsteak's purt
    near done,
But all the chawin' teeth I've got's a little over one.
Ol' Gus shore savvies cookin' steak—I'd like to eat a pound,
But heck, I couldn't chaw it if he took and had it ground!
You talk about Thanksgivin,' boys, and here you see me set,
A plumb wore out old cowhand; but I'm mighty thankful yet
For every horse I've ever rode, and every sight I've saw—
But most of all for *gravy*—which a man don't have to chawl"

BROWN SAUCE

3 tablespoons butter
2 onions chopped
½ cup diced celery
1 clove garlic crushed
½ teaspoon dry mustard
½ teaspoon salt

¼ teaspoon pepper
3 tablespoons flour
2 cups beef stock
1 tablespoon Worcestershire
    sauce
¼ cup Madeira

Heat the butter; add the onions, celery, garlic, mustard, salt and
pepper. Cook 5 minutes. Add flour, made into a paste with a little
stock. Add the stock, Worcestershire sauce and Madeira. Simmer
over low heat for half an hour. Strain. A tasty basic sauce, good
for pot roast or roast beef.

SPECIAL STEAK SAUCE

½ Spanish onion chopped
2 slices bacon
1 teaspoon butter
½ pound mushrooms cut up
½ teaspoon salt

1 (10½ ounce) can tomato
    soup
⅛ teaspoon pepper
½ teaspoon prepared mus-
    tard

Fry the onion and diced bacon in butter until the onion is soft
and the bacon crisp. Add mushrooms, cover and simmer for 2 to 3
minutes. Add the salt, soup, pepper and mustard and heat together.
For steak and hamburger.

SOUR CREAM ROQUEFORT

¼ cup sour cream
2 ounces Roquefort cheese

½ teaspoon Worcestershire sauce
¼ teaspoon dry mustard

Mix all of the ingredients together thoroughly. May be spread on broiled beef, or served with hamburger or steak.

They had a code on the old frontier,
And most oldtimers heeded it.
They never did hang a man, I hear,
Unless they thought he needed it.

CATTLEMAN SAUCE

½ pound mushrooms minced
2 large onions chopped
2 green peppers chopped fine
2 sweet peppers chopped fine
4 cloves garlic crushed
2 stalks celery chopped fine
3 tablespoons bacon fat
2 (1 pound) cans tomatoes

2 (1 pound) cans tomato purée
1 pint wine vinegar
½ pound sugar
3 tablespoons Worcestershire sauce
1 teaspoon Tabasco sauce
2 tablespoons salt
½ teaspoon pepper
½ teaspoon cayenne pepper
½ cup dry mustard

Mix the mushrooms, onions, peppers, garlic and celery and sauté in the bacon fat. Mash the tomatoes and mix with the tomato purée. Reduce the wine vinegar and sugar by boiling. Pour this very carefully into the tomato mixture—it will spatter. Mix this with the sautéed vegetables and season with the rest of the ingredients. Simmer for 1 hour.

BROWN WINE SAUCE

3 tablespoons butter
2 tablespoons flour
1 cup beef broth

⅓ cup sherry or Madeira
½ teaspoon salt
¼ teaspoon pepper

Cook the butter until light brown. Stir in the flour and cook until light brown. Add the broth slowly while stirring. Boil 3 minutes, add the wine, salt and pepper and boil another minute or two.

BROWN WINE HORSERADISH SAUCE

½ recipe Brown Wine
  Sauce*
2 tablespoons sour cream

3 tablespoons prepared
  horseradish

Mix the horseradish and sour cream and stir into the wine sauce.

BEARNAISE SAUCE

¼ cup white wine
½ cup wine or tarragon vinegar
1 tablespoon minced shallots
  or scallions
1 teaspoon chervil

2 tablespoons minced tar-
  ragon
3 egg yolks
⅔ cup butter
1 tablespoon minced parsley
¼ teaspoon salt
⅛ teaspoon pepper

Boil the wine, vinegar, shallots or scallions, chervil and 1 tablespoon tarragon until reduced to half and slightly thickened. Cool,
strain and put into a double boiler. Add the slightly beaten egg
yolks and 1 tablespoon water. Beat until the mixture is light and
fluffy. Add a fourth of the butter at a time while stirring. Add
remaining tarragon and the parsley, salt and pepper.

HUNTER'S SAUCE

½ cup coarsely chopped
  onion
1 cup sliced mushrooms
2 tablespoons oil
¼ cup butter
1 cup red wine
½ cups tomato purée
1 cup Brown Sauce* or
  canned brown gravy

1 cup chopped tomatoes
1 clove garlic crushed
½ teaspoon basil
1 tablespoon minced pars-
  ley
1 tablespoon minced chives
1 teaspoon salt
⅛ teaspoon pepper

Sauté the onion and mushrooms in oil and 1 tablespoon butter
for about 5 minutes. Add wine and reduce to half. Add tomato
purée and Brown Sauce and simmer 15 minutes. In a separate pan,
sauté tomatoes, garlic and basil in 1 tablespoon butter. Just before
serving, add parsley and chives and combine tomato mixture with
the sauce. Add salt, pepper and remaining 2 tablespoons butter.

She married a cowboy. He keeps her awake
With sounds that are hard to excuse.
He's been around cows so much that she vows
Instead of just snoring, he moos!

SPICY SAUCE

2 tablespoons oil
1 (10½ ounce) can tomato
    soup
1 onion grated
2 tablespoons vinegar
2 teaspoons brown sugar
1 tablespoon soy sauce

1 teaspoon celery seed
½ teaspoon cayenne pepper
¼ teaspoon ground cumin
    seed (optional)
⅛ teaspoon spice Parisienne
    (optional)

Mix all of the ingredients with ½ cup water and heat together until well blended.

SWEET-SOUR SAUCE

¼ cup brown sugar
¼ cup prepared mustard
¼ cup molasses
¼ cup vinegar

¼ cup Worcestershire sauce
½ cup pineapple juice
½ teaspoon lemon juice

Mix the sugar, mustard and molasses. Add vinegar, Worcestershire sauce, pineapple juice and lemon juice. Mix this all very thoroughly and heat. Serve hot.

MUSHROOM SAUCE

1 small onion minced
½ to ¾ pound mushrooms
    sliced
2 tablespoons butter
2 tablespoons flour

½ cup consommé
½ cup milk
½ teaspoon salt
¼ teaspoon pepper
⅛ teaspoon lemon juice

Brown the onion and mushrooms in butter. Blend in the flour and stir in the consommé slowly. Add the milk, salt and pepper and simmer 5 minutes. Stir in the lemon juice and remove from heat. Especially good for steak.

ANCHOVY SAUCE

4 anchovies minced or 2 teaspoons anchovy paste
1 small onion minced
2 tablespoons dry mustard

1 (10¾ ounce) can beef gravy or 2 tablespoons butter,
2 tablespoons flour, and
1 cup beef broth, or 1 cup water and 2 bouillon cubes

Mix the anchovy, onion and mustard. If using canned gravy, add this and heat together. If making the brown sauce, melt the butter, blend in the flour and, when browned, add beef broth or water and bouillon cubes slowly while stirring. When smooth and thickened, add the anchovy mixture and heat together.

MUSTARD SAUCE

2 tablespoons prepared mustard
½ cup heavy cream
½ teaspoon salt

⅛ teaspoon paprika
⅛ teaspoon curry powder
½ teaspoon sugar

Mix all of the ingredients together and heat but do not boil.

CURRY SAUCE

1 small onion chopped fine
2 tablespoons butter
1 tablespoon flour
1 to 2 tablespoons curry powder

½ teaspoon salt
⅛ teaspoon pepper
2 cups chicken broth or consommé

Sauté the onion in butter until transparent. Add flour, 1 tablespoon curry, salt and pepper and blend. Add the broth slowly while stirring. Simmer for 15 minutes until thick. Add more curry to taste.

CURRY BECHAMEL SAUCE

1 small onion minced
½ clove garlic crushed
2 tablespoons butter
3 tablespoons flour
1 tablespoon curry powder

½ teaspoon salt
Pinch white pepper
¾ cup chicken broth
½ cup light cream

Sauté the onion and garlic in butter until onion is golden. Stir in the flour, curry, salt and pepper. At this point it helps to cook the flour and butter very slowly before adding the broth slowly while stirring. Add the cream and cook only until thickened and smooth. Strain.

FRUITED CURRY SAUCE

1 onion minced
2 tablespoons butter or margarine
1 tablespoon flour
1 to 2 tablespoons curry powder
½ teaspoon salt
1 cup consommé

3 tomatoes peeled and chopped or 1 cup canned
1 banana sliced
1 large apple peeled and chopped
½ cup blanched raisins
⅓ cup shredded coconut

Sauté the onion in butter until transparent but not brown. Add the flour, mixed with curry powder and salt. Stir and add consommé. Simmer 2 or 3 minutes. Then add the remaining ingredients and simmer 20 minutes. If the sauce is too thick, add a little water, consommé or tomato juice.

MEAT SAUCE FOR SPAGHETTI

1 pound ground beef
2 onions chopped
1 clove garlic crushed
3 tablespooons salad or olive oil
1 (6 ounce) can tomato paste
1 (1 pound 3 ounce) can tomatoes

1 teaspoon salt
½ teaspoon pepper
½ teaspoon sugar
½ teaspoon cinnamon
½ teaspoon orégano
1 bay leaf crumbled

Brown the onion and garlic in oil. Add tomato paste, tomatoes and the beef. Stir and simmer, covered, for half an hour. Add the remaining ingredients and simmer gently for another hour.

Don't expect that the chuck wagon boss, just because he can straddle a horse, will ever serve horseradish sauce!

SOUR CREAM HORSERADISH SAUCE

¼ cup prepared horseradish
1 cup sour cream

½ teaspoon salt

Mix the ingredients together thoroughly. Especially good with boiled beef.

WHIPPED CREAM HORSERADISH SAUCE

¼ cup prepared horseradish
½ cup heavy cream whipped
½ teaspoon salt

Few drops Tabasco or
Worcestershire sauce
(optional)

Mix the drained horseradish into the whipped cream and season with salt and Tabasco. Good with all beef.

CURRY HORSERADISH SAUCE

½ cup heavy cream
1 tablespoon prepared horseradish
1 tablespoon prepared mustard

1 tablespoon curry powder
1 clove garlic crushed or ⅛
   teaspoon garlic powder
½ teaspoon salt

Whip the cream and blend in the drained horseradish, the mustard, curry powder, garlic and salt. Especially good on cold roast beef or cold steak.

If you frequently serve barbecued beef to 1500 of your intimate friends, you will appreciate having the following recipe from The Cattleman in New York City:

BAR B Q SAUCE

5 gallons onions chopped
   very fine
5 pounds bacon chopped
   very fine
2 cups salt
2 cups soya sauce
6 #10 cans tomato purée
2 gallons cider vinegar
½ cup chili powder
3 pounds English mustard

1 cup paprika
2½ teaspoons cayenne pepper
2 cups corn syrup
½ #10 can molasses
2 pounds brown sugar
12 bay leaves
5 ounces liquid smoke
5 #10 cans water
1 pound garlic

Mix all together in a bathtub.

If you lead a less crowded life, you'll love this reduced version:

CATTLEMAN BAR B Q SAUCE

4 slices bacon diced
2 onions minced
1½ teaspoons salt
2 teaspoons soy sauce
3 cups tomato purée
1 teaspoon chili powder
¼ cup dry mustard
2 teaspoons paprika
⅛ teaspoon cayenne
2 tablespoons dark corn
   syrup
½ cup molasses
¼ cup brown sugar
1 bay leaf
2 tablespoons liquid smoke
2 cloves garlic

Sauté the bacon and onions in a large pot. Add all of the remaining ingredients and simmer for an hour.

TEXAS BARBECUE SAUCE

¼ cup vinegar
⅔ cup catchup
1 teaspoon prepared mustard
1 teaspoon Worcestershire
   sauce
6 drops Tabasco sauce
1 clove garlic crushed
2 tablespoons orange juice
1 teaspoon sugar
⅛ teaspoon salt

Mix all of the ingredients together thoroughly.

HONEY BARBECUE SAUCE

1 cup catchup
1 onion minced
¼ cup vinegar
1 teaspoon paprika
2 tablespoons dry mustard
1 clove garlic crushed
1 teaspoon chili powder
3 tablespoons honey

Mix the ingredients with 1 cup water and simmer slowly for half an hour.

CHILI-SAUCE BARBECUE SAUCE

½ cup chopped onion
2 tablespoons bacon fat
1 tablespoon Worcestershire
   sauce
¼ cup lemon juice
1 (12 ounce) bottle chili
   sauce
½ teaspoon salt
¼ teaspoon paprika
1 tablespoon dry mustard
1 tablespoon Kitchen Bouquet

Brown the onion in the bacon fat. Add ½ cup water and stir in the remaining ingredients. Simmer a minute or two.

Chuck wagons ain't as common now as once they used to be
On ranch and range in them old days, so rugged, raw and free.
But there are still oldtimers whose gray heads can well recall
Times when the old chuck wagon was the cowboy's all in all.
They just called it "the Wagon" on the roundup or the trail.
The kitchen of the cowboy was that chuck box on its tail.
This chuck box was the cupboard where the coosie kept the gear
With which he wrangled rations for the cowpoke cavalier
Who came in off the cow work, like a farmer to his shack,
To save his hungry stomach from a-growin' to his back.
He might get whistle-berries and shotgun-waddin' bread,
It might be beef and biscuits, but it got the cowhand fed.

Chuck wasn't all the Wagon meant to sons of saddle sweat:
It meant dry clothes, a bed, a fire, and somewhere he could set
To do what little talkin' that a cowboy's life allows
About the things he's thought about while out there with the cows.
'Twas where his comrades brought him, was he sick or banged up bad.
'Twas his refuge and his haven. 'Twas the only home he had.
Out there upon the cow range far away from any town,
The Wagon was the cowboy's friend that never let him down.
So when he throwed his bedroll in the Wagon for a "work,"
It meant he'd sworn allegiance to a job he'd never shirk.
They asked me "What's the Wagon?" . . . It's a thing you can't explain
Unless you've bedded 'round one under stars out on the plain.
Two riders, meetin' on the range, would hail—like passin' ships—
And "Whichaway's the Wagon?" was the question on their lips.
So when a cowboy's time has come, Saint Pete will hear his hail:
"Hey! Whichaway's the Wagon?" . . . And He'll point him up the Trail.

BEER BARBECUE SAUCE

1 cup catchup
1 cup chili sauce
½ cup prepared mustard
½ cup brown sugar
1 tablespoon freshly ground
   pepper
Few drops Tabasco sauce
2 tablespoons salad oil

½ cup white wine vinegar
Juice of 1 lemon
2 tablespoons Worcestershire
   sauce
1 tablespoon soy sauce
1 clove garlic crushed
1 (12 ounce) can beer

Mix the ingredients and stir in the beer after the sauce is thoroughly blended. This recipe may be cut in half for 4 to 6 people.

SOY BARBECUE SAUCE

¾ cup soy sauce
1 clove garlic crushed
¼ cup white wine

½ teaspoon ginger or 1 tablespoon minced

Heat together for 2 minutes. This may also be used as a marinade.

BRANDY BARBECUE SAUCE

¼ cup honey
½ cup soy sauce
2 tablespoons brown sugar
1 teaspoon salt

¼ teaspoon pepper
1 teaspoon garlic powder
Few drops Tabasco sauce
¼ cup brandy

Heat the honey, soy sauce and brown sugar with ½ cup water until the honey and sugar are dissolved. Mix thoroughly with the remaining ingredients. You may use this sauce to brush on meat for the last half hour of cooking if you wish.

STEAK BUTTER

1 teaspoon prepared
   mustard
1 tablespoon catchup
Juice of ½ lemon

1 tablespoon Worcestershire
   sauce
½ pound creamed butter

Mix all ingredients thoroughly together.

PARSLEY BUTTER (MAITRE D'HOTEL)

½ cup butter
1 tablespoon lemon juice
1 tablespoon minced parsley

¼ teaspoon salt
⅛ teaspoon pepper

Cream the butter; add the lemon juice a few drops at a time, then add the rest of the ingredients. Keep cool (do not refrigerate) until ready to serve. Especially good with broiled steak.

GARLIC BUTTER

6 cloves garlic
½ cup butter

¼ teaspoon salt
Pinch white pepper

Boil the peeled garlic for 5 minutes. Cream the butter. Put the garlic through a press or pound to a purée and work it into the butter with the salt and pepper.

BERCY BUTTER

4 shallots
½ cup white wine
½ cup butter

1 tablespoon minced parsley
¼ teaspoon salt
¼ teaspoon freshly ground
  pepper

Peel and chop the shallots fine. Boil in wine for 5 minutes. Cool. Cream the butter, add the shallots and wine a little at a time, then add the parsley, salt and pepper. Recommended for broiled beef.

HORSERADISH BUTTER

1 tablespoon freshly ground
  horseradish

¼ cup butter

Cream together.

CHIVE BUTTER

¼ pound butter
2 tablespoons minced chives

2 teaspoons lemon juice

Cream the butter and blend in the chives and lemon juice.

WINE BUTTER

1 cup red wine
1 shallot minced
¼ teaspoon salt
¼ teaspoon freshly ground
  pepper

Pinch sugar
Few drops lemon juice
1 teaspoon minced parsley
¼ cup creamed butter

Simmer the wine, shallot, salt, pepper, sugar and lemon juice together until the wine is reduced about one-third. Remove from heat and chill. Blend into the creamed butter.

MUSTARD BUTTER

¼ pound butter
Salt

2 tablespoons prepared
  mustard

Soften the butter and stir in the mustard until well blended. Add a little salt to taste.

Not often, but once in a while a dude ranch guest from the East betrays a little condescension toward the natives. On one occasion a veddy, veddy aristocratic lady from Boston was trying to impress the folks at the Ox Bow Ranch with a bit of genetic information.

"You must understand," she said, "that back in Boston, family is the all important consideration in the choice of our associates. The main thing we are interested in is *breeding!*"

"Yes ma'am," drawled Brazos Bill. "We enjoy it out here in the West, too. But *somebody* always has to take time off to do the cooking."

LEMON MARINADE FOR STEAK

1 cup olive oil
½ teaspoon salt
¾ teaspoon freshly ground
  pepper

Juice of 1 large lemon
1 clove garlic

Mix the oil, salt, pepper and lemon juice. If you want to taste the garlic, rub the steak on both sides with the clove, which has been cut in half. For a whiff of garlic only, cut the clove into pieces and drop it into the mixture. Put the steak in the marinade and let stand for 12 to 24 hours at room temperature. Grill as usual. Use the marinade to fry onions, potatoes, or something; don't throw it away.

MARINADE WITH GARLIC

1 cup olive oil
1 cup wine vinegar
1 clove garlic crushed

2 teaspoons salt
½ teaspoon pepper

Mix all ingredients together.

FRENCH DRESSING MARINADE

1 cup olive oil
⅓ cup wine vinegar
1½ teaspoons salt
¼ teaspoon pepper

¼ teaspoon paprika
½ teaspoon sugar
½ teaspoon dry mustard

Mix all ingredients together.

OIL MARINADE

½ cup olive oil
⅓ cup soy sauce

1 clove garlic cut up

Mix the ingredients together.

BUTTER MARINADE THAT DOUBLES FOR SAUCE

1 cup melted butter
2 tablespoons lemon juice
1 clove garlic crushed

1 teaspoon salt
2 tablespoons minced parsley

Mix all ingredients together.

CATCHUP BUTTER MARINADE AND SAUCE

½ cup butter
¼ cup olive oil
½ cup catchup
Juice of 1 lemon
1 teaspoon prepared mustard
1 teaspoon Worcestershire
    sauce

1 clove garlic crushed
    (optional)
1 medium onion finely
    minced
1 teaspoon salt
¼ teaspoon freshly ground
    pepper

Mix all ingredients together.

Now here is the recipe, time-tried and true,
For chuck wagon coffee, the buckaroo's brew:
Use Arbuckle's Roasted, in case you can get it;
Pour in enough water to just sort of wet it.
Boil hard for an hour, then into it toss
The well rusted shoe off a clubfooted hoss;
Gaze into the pot for a few minutes steady—
If the hoss shoe is floating, your coffee is ready!

INDEX